God Divided
the Nations

God Divided the Nations
© 1998 by Noah W. Hutchings

Printed in the United States of America

ISBN 1-57558-024-1

Cover design by Christi Killian

God Divided the Nations

Dr. Noah W. Hutchings

Hearthstone Publishing, Ltd.
Oklahoma City, Oklahoma

About the Author

Noah Hutchings is president of the Southwest Radio Church, one of the foremost prophetic ministries in the world. He has written dozens of books and booklets on prophecy and other Bible themes. Pastor Hutchings has been active in missions and communications ministries for more than 40 years and is recognized for being a world traveler, having led tours to Israel, Iraq, Egypt, Europe, China, and other nations around the world. His plain and conversational style of writing makes the subject matter he approaches both interesting and informative to the reader, regardless of the level of education or understanding.

Table of Contents

Chapter 1

The Edenic Age

God that made the world and all things therein, seeing that he is Lord of heaven and earth, dwelleth not
in temples made with hands; Neither is worshipped
with men's hands, as though he needed any thing,
seeing he giveth to all life, and breath, and all things;
And hath made of one blood all nations of men for to
dwell on all the face of the earth, and hath determined
the times before appointed, and the bounds of their
habitation.

—Acts 17:24–26

Scripture affirms that mankind is divided into nations, races, and languages according to the will of God, so that His purpose for man and the earth might be fulfilled. The Apostle Paul declared that God not only brought about this separation, but He created boundaries so that the nations would stay divided.

One of the seeming enigmas of our time is why God split the human race into nations, because there have been an estimated 600 million people killed in the wars of history over the past five thousand years. As staggering as these casualty figures appear, they tell only a part of the shameful story. To the loss of life must be added the destruction of cities, the loss of property, the tax burden on the masses to support war, and the untold sufferings due to injuries, the breakup of homes, and separation from loved ones. As lamentable as the chronicles of war are, concerning man's inhumanity to man, there is even less hope for the immediate future. For the first time in history the nations now have the capability to destroy all life on Earth and return this planet to its primeval condition described in Genesis 1:2: ". . . the earth was without form, and void; and darkness was upon the face of the deep."

The "prince of this world" has, at this very hour, the necessary power within the armed forces of the nations to destroy in one hour what God created in six days. Why did God divide mankind into nations in the first place? And why is God silent as the world teeters on the brink of extinction? For the answer to these and other questions relative to our subject, we go back to the beginning as recorded in the first two chapters of our Bible.

Moses recorded in Genesis 1:1: "In the beginning God created the heaven and the earth." The Apostle Paul, in accordance with the revelation given to him by Jesus Christ, amplified Moses' declaration by stating further: "Through faith we understand that the worlds were framed by the word of God, so that things which are seen were not made of things which do appear" (Heb. 11:3).

Matter exists in eternity in the form of power, or energy, and God dwells in eternity (Isa. 57:15). When, "in the beginning" God spoke, matter appeared. The phrase "in the beginning" has reference to time. Time began, matter appeared. Scientists in our generation now theorize that all matter in the universe from which the galaxies, suns, and planets were formed, came into being in one ten-thousandeth of a second, or less. They call it the "Big Bang" theory.

Scientific evolutionists have theorized the "Big Bang" theory to try to explain the existence of matter, but they have yet to come up with a theory that explains space and time. What if someone asked, "How did you get that new car in your driveway?" Then you replied: "There was a bang and it just happened."

"In the beginning God created . . ." (Gen. 1:1). The Word does not say that "in the beginning God began to create. . . ." All the creation, and making things of the things that were created, ended with the sixth day. Since sin entered the world through Adam, everything that God created has been deteriorating because of sin (Rom. 8:19–21). The second law of thermodynamics, *entropy*, dictates that the universal system is running down. The earth is not as productive as it once was; there is not as much oxygen in the air as there once was; the animals are not as large as they once were; the hydrogen supply on the sun is less every day, etc.

In the first two chapters of Genesis Moses recorded in detail God's creative acts in bringing into being all plant and animal life on the Earth. Then, God made man on the sixth day. It is important to our subject to know how God made man and to what end he was created.

The name for the first man, *Adam,* in the Hebrew means "of the ground," or "taken out of the red earth." Only man was created in the image of God, indicating a tripartite being. An animal has a body and soul. The soul expresses personality, or being. In numerous scriptures the writer declares that his soul is happy, sad, joyful, etc. Animals have souls in that a dog can express pleasure, anger, sadness, and other emotions. Owners become attached to their pets for this reason. Our soul identifies us as a distinct personality apart from others, but man was created a unique being in that he was made in the image of God, and the Creator breathed into the first man, Adam, the "breath of life" (Gen. 2:7). Man was created body, soul, and spirit. Adam could have eaten of the Tree of Life and lived as he was created—forever. Such a promise was not committed to any other form of life on the earth.

Adam was created a complete personality—one being (Gen. 5:1–2). While every part of God's creation was good of itself, God perceived that it was not good for Adam to live by himself in the Garden of Eden. And so in Genesis 2:20–24, we read about the first division of / the human race.

> And Adam gave names to all cattle, and to the fowl of the air, and to every beast of the field; but for Adam there was not found an help meet for him. And the LORD God caused a deep sleep to fall upon Adam, and he slept: and he took one of his ribs, and closed up the flesh instead thereof; And the rib, which the LORD God had taken from man, made he a woman, and brought her unto the man. And Adam said, This is now bone of my bones, and flesh of my flesh: she shall be called Woman, because **she was taken out of Man.** Therefore shall a man leave his father and his mother, and shall cleave unto his wife: and **they shall be one flesh.**

The first dividing of man came because of the love and compassion of God for Adam. The personality of Adam was divided. Eve was taken out of Adam. When the two parts were united in the first marriage, they again became one person. The husband and the wife, united in God's complete will and purpose for marriage, can and should become "as one." Man by himself is only half a person, and the same is true of the woman.

The only thing that God said was wrong with His creation after the sixth day was that man was alone. God is love and He made man to love, but there was no choice in love for man to make. While Adam doubtless loved both God and Eve, Adam's priorities were misplaced. God's Word is always supreme, absolute, and eternal.

The Second Division

The second division of the human race, and the reason for it, is recorded in Genesis 4:8–17.

> And Cain talked with Abel his brother: and it came to pass, when they were in the field, that Cain rose up against Abel his brother, and slew him. And the LORD said unto Cain, Where is Abel thy brother? And he said, I know not: Am I my brother's keeper? And he said, What hast thou done? the voice of thy brother's blood crieth unto me from the ground. And now art thou cursed from the earth, which hath opened her mouth to receive thy brother's blood from thy hand; When thou tillest the ground, it shall not henceforth yield unto thee her strength; a fugitive and a vagabond shalt thou be in the earth. And Cain said unto the LORD, My punishment is greater than I can bear. Behold, thou hast driven me out this day from the face of the earth; and from thy face shall I be hid; and I shall be a fugitive and a vagabond in the earth; and it shall come to pass, that every one that findeth me shall slay me. And the LORD said unto him, Therefore whosoever slayeth Cain, vengeance shall be taken on him sevenfold. And the LORD set a mark upon Cain, lest any finding him should kill him.

And Cain went out from the presence of the LORD, and dwelt in the land of Nod, on the east of Eden. And Cain knew his wife; and she conceived, and bare Enoch: and he builded a city, and called the name of the city, after the name of his son, Enoch.

Cain was driven out from the presence of Adam and Eve and the society of that day. He went to live in the land of Nod. He was separated, and his descendants were segregated, because of sin. In the Hebrew, *Nod* means "wandering," indicating that he led a nomadic existence. Nevertheless, Cain must have taken his wife with him. In the due course of time, his family grew in numbers and Cain founded a city. Although there were no identifiable nations in the Antediluvian society, in the fourth chapter of Genesis we are told the following about that society:

Vs. 17: *"Cain . . . builded a city."*—There were cities.

Vs. 20: *"And Adah bare Jabal: he was the father of such as dwell in tents, and of such as have cattle."*— There were farmers and ranchers.

Vs. 21: *"And his brother's name was Jubal: he was the father of all such as handle the harp and organ."*— There were musicians, and doubtless other types of art.

Vs. 22: *"And Zillah, she also bare Tubal-cain, an instructer of every artificer in brass and iron."*— There were foundries and probably factories.

On page 78 of *Halley's Bible Handbook* there is an archaeological note concerning the location of many of the pre-Flood cities. We quote:

The Field Museum-Oxford University Joint Expedition, under the direction of Dr. Stephen Langdon, found a bed of clean water-laid clay, in a lower strata of the ruins of Kish, 5 feet thick, indicating a flood of vast proportions. It contained no objects of any kind. Underneath it the relics represented an entirely different type of culture. Among the relics found was a four-wheeled Chariot, the wheels made of wood and copper nails, with the skeletons of the animals that drew it. . . . Underneath the flood deposit was a layer of charcoal and ashes, a dark colored culture refuse which may have been wall remains, painted pottery, skeletons, cylinder seals, stamp seals, pots, pans and vessels. . . .

From Adam and Eve came sons and daughters, and we read in Genesis 6:1, "And it came to pass, when men began to multiply on the face of the earth, and daughters were born unto them." Men and women lived to be eight and nine hundred years of age; therefore, the population of the earth rapidly increased. One of the common questions asked about this earliest age in man's history is: "Where did Cain get his wife?" It is obvious that he married a sister, a niece, a cousin, or another near female relative. Before the Flood, God did not put on the conscience of man that it was wrong to marry within the family. The law against marrying close relatives did not come until God gave Moses the commandments.

Therefore, as the population increased over the face of the earth, cities were built and the human race began to congregate into cities and principalities. However, there was no government to rule over man or restrain his lust or greed. Lamech killed two men and boasted that if Cain could get away with murder, so could he (Gen. 4:23–24).

The First Curse

It is written in Genesis 3:8 that the Lord God would come down to the Garden of Eden and have fellowship with Adam and Eve. This was the purpose for which man was created—to love God and have communion with Him, not because man had to, but because he chose to. This is why God is calling a people out of this world for His name. The church, the completed body, will fulfill the plan and purpose that God had for man in the beginning. We read in Ephesians 1:3–5:

> Blessed be the God and Father of our Lord Jesus Christ, who hath blessed us with all spiritual blessings in heavenly places in Christ: According as he hath chosen us in him before the foundation of the world, that we should be holy and without blame before him in love: Having predestinated us unto the adoption of children by Jesus Christ to himself, according to the good pleasure of his will.

But the first man and the first woman severed their fellowship with God when they exercised their free wills to disobey Him and depend upon their own knowledge. And just as the first dividing of the society of man came because of sin, so did the first curse on creation.

The Garden of Eden must have been an immense jungle of vegetation and animal life. The general area, as evidenced by the junction of the Euphrates and the Tigris rivers, was somewhere in the Persian Gulf near Kuwait. Oil is the residue of the decomposition of animal and vegetable matter, and there is more oil under the ground in that area than in any other place in the world.

The breakup of the land mass of the world after Babel was to help keep the nations divided, and the following description of the Antediluvian earth given by Josephus agrees with Scripture:

> Moses says further, that God planted a paradise in the east, flourishing with all sorts of trees; and that among them was the tree of life, and another of knowledge, whereby was to be known what was good and evil; and that when he brought Adam and his wife into this garden, he commanded them to take care of the plants. Now the garden was watered by one river, which ran round about the whole earth, and was parted into four parts. And Phison, which denotes a multitude, running into India, makes its exit into the sea, and is by the Greeks called Ganges. Euphrates also, as well as Tigris, goes down into the Red Sea. Now the name Euphrates, or Phrath, denotes either a dispersion, or a flower: by Tigris, or Diglath, is signified what is swift, with narrowness; and Geon runs through Egypt, and denotes what arises from the east, which the Greeks call Nile.

Later in the series, we will discuss how the Ganges and the Nile became separated from the Tigris and Euphrates. Also, in the Antediluvian age, there was an even temperature over all the land area, and the water which came down at the Flood was above the earth. It was probably in a frozen ice form much like the rings around Saturn. Our latest space probe to Saturn discovered that Saturn's rings were composed of billions of huge chunks of ice.

Before the Flood it was unnecessary for men to eat meat, because the nuts and herbs were delicious and nutritious. Adam was told in Genesis 1:29 that the herbs, the seeds, and the fruit of the trees "shall be for meat." The word "meat" in the Hebrew actually means "protein." If the world was restored to its Edenic condition, many of the reasons why nations war against each other today would be resolved. There would be food, shelter, and clothing for everyone. However, when sin entered, God had to change creation for man's own good. The Tree of Life was taken away to keep man from eating of it and living forever in a sinful state separated from His Creator. Likewise, the rest of the plant and animal life was affected. God spoke to Adam in Genesis 3:17–18:

> . . . Because thou hast hearkened unto the voice of thy wife, and hast eaten of the tree, of which I commanded thee, saying, Thou shalt not eat of it: cursed is the ground for thy sake; in sorrow shalt thou eat of it all the days of thy life; Thorns also and thistles shall it bring forth to thee; and thou shalt eat the herb of the field.

When men become affluent, and have an abundance of food, they forget God. Over and over Israel was warned not to forget that it was God who gave them food, clothing, and shelter. Only when God withholds rain and causes the ground to withhold the necessary elements to sustain life will men acknowledge the Lord and cry for help. It was for man's own good that the first curse came upon the creation. And it was in the Garden of Eden, when sin first came into the world through Adam, that God's plan and purpose for dividing mankind into languages, races, and nations began to unfold.

Chapter 2

The Antediluvian Society

In continuing our quest for information and answers as to how and why God divided the nations, we consider again the Antediluvian social order. We have already brought out that after Adam and Eve sinned, the Edenic creation was cursed for man's sake. Mutations occurred in the plant life and the environment to produce conditions which made it necessary for man to struggle to earn his bread, and at the same time other mutations brought forth disease germs that caused illness and death. The thistles, burrs, deserts, droughts, famines, and disease came because of sin. Just as the first sin brought on the first curse, exceeding sin produced the second curse. We read again in Genesis 4:11–12:

> And now art thou cursed from the earth, which hath opened her mouth to receive thy brother's blood from thy hand; When thou tillest the ground, it shall not henceforth yield unto thee her strength; a fugitive and a vagabond shalt thou be in the earth.

God told Adam that he would have to till the ground and earn his living from the sweat of his brow; and Cain was informed that even when he worked and sweated, the ground would produce only a meager living. Because of Cain's sin, hardships would follow—droughts and famines. However, the environment before the Flood, even after the second curse, was much better than today. Josephus wrote on this subject in *Antiquities of the Jews,* chapter 3, book 1:

> Now when Noah had lived three hundred and fifty years after the Flood, and that all that time happily, he died, having lived the number of nine hundred and fifty years: but let no one, upon comparing the lives of the ancients with our lives, and with the few years which we now live, think that what we have said of them is false; or make the shortness of our lives at present an argument that neither did they attain to so long a duration of life; for those ancients were beloved of God and [lately] made by God himself; and because their food was then fitter for the prolongation of life, might well live so great a number of years; and besides, God afforded them a longer time of life on account of their virtue and the good use they made of it in astronomical and geometrical discoveries, which would not have afforded the time of foretelling [the periods of the stars] unless they had lived six hundred years; for the Great Year is completed in that interval.

The Antediluvians, especially those of the godly line of Seth, lived to be several hundred years of age according to Scripture and the Jewish historian Josephus. The descendants of Seth were exceedingly wise men who studied astronomy, and they understood God's plan and purpose for the ages which was revealed in the stars. According to Josephus, they recorded this knowledge in a great monument of stone in the land of Siriad. The land of Siriad is that part of Egypt in which the Great Pyramid of Giza was built. The Great Pyramid was built upon mathematical equations and knowledge of astronomy that was thought to have been discovered first by the Greeks, but the most common date given for the erection of the Great Pyramid is 2,700 B.C., or several hundred years before the Flood.

In spite of the second curse placed upon creation, the society of the Antediluvian age prospered. We read of this time from page 70 of *Halley's Bible Handbook:*

> While Adam was yet living his descendants learned the use of copper and iron, and invented musical instruments. Until recently the use of iron was thought to have been unknown previous to the 12th century B.C. . . . In 1933, Dr. H. E. Frankfort, of the Oriental Institute, discovered, in the ruins of Asmar, about 100 miles northeast of Babylon, an Iron blade which had been made about 2700 B.C.; thus pushing back the known use of iron some 1,500 years. Primitive inscriptions have revealed that Babylonia [which includes the site of the Garden of Eden] has never been inhabited with people unacquainted with the use of metals. Copper instruments have been found in the ruins of a number of pre-Flood cities. The Weld Prism, which gives names of ten long-lived kings who reigned before the Flood, says the 3rd, 5th, and 6th reigned in "Badgurgurru." This word means "city of workers in bronze." It may be a tradition of Cain's city.

The Line of Seth

After Cain had been banished from the inhabited

region of the earth at that time, we read in Genesis 4:25–26:

> And Adam knew his wife again; and she bare a son, and called his name Seth: For God, said she, hath appointed me another seed instead of Abel, whom Cain slew. And to Seth, to him also there was born a son; and he called his name Enos: then began men to call upon the name of the LORD.

The name for *Seth* in the Hebrew means "compensation, or substituted." God compensated Eve for the loss of Abel. Abel was righteous because of faith in the sacrifice of the lamb, which looked forward to Jesus Christ. Likewise, we have reason to believe that Seth was also a godly man. God would not have compensated Eve for Abel had Seth been ungodly.

Seth named his first son *Enos*, which means "moral—born to die." The name means that although men are made righteous before God through the new birth, the carnal flesh must decay. God told Adam that in the day he transgressed His commandment and ate of the tree of the knowledge of good and evil, he would surely die. There are two explanations of this curse:

1. Adam did die spiritually when he was cut off from God.
2. Adam, nor any man since, has ever lived to be a thousand years old in the flesh. A day is as a thousand years with the Lord, and a thousand years as a day.

Some scholars disagree as to what the text of Genesis 4:26 means—the scripture says that after the birth of Enos, "then began men to call upon the name of the

Lord." *The Pentateuch and Haftorahs—The Hebrew Text,* English translation and commentary by Chief Rabbi Dr. J. H. Hertz, said of this verse:

> Then men began to pray to God; or, once more call upon God under the name Adonai, Lord, which seems to have been forgotten among the descendants of Cain.

D. W. Bullinger says of the same scripture:

> Men did not begin to worship [or pray], for Abel worshipped, and others, doubtless, long before. But here, the Scripture means they began to call upon [their gods] by the name of Jehovah. Enos, though a son of Seth, is included here because he went in the way of Cain.

Both explanations are possible, because it was soon after this that all flesh became corrupt, and every man did what was right in his own eyes, except one man, Noah. In the line of Seth there were many men of faith like Mahalaleel (whose name meant "God is Splendour") and Enoch which means "walked with God." Enoch was 365 years old at the time of his translation to heaven. Another man in the line of Seth was Methuselah, whose name meant "it shall be sent." Without doubt, the name meaning "it shall be sent" looked forward to the Flood. Chronology indicates that Methuselah died the year the Flood came, and he was the oldest man who ever lived. Methuselah's testimony augmented the preaching of Noah that the Flood was going to come.

The human race before the Flood was all of one language and one race. While it seems evident there were social and economic classes, and even leaders of cities called kings, there were no governmental divisions and little or no governmental restraint. Men continued to be strong and virile even at seven and eight hundred years of age, and women continued to be beautiful, strong, and childbearing at the same age. We do not know how many children that Adam and Eve had— possibly a hundred or more. The Scripture simply says that they had sons and daughters. If the names of all their children had been recorded it would possibly take an hour to read all their names, and our Bible would be much larger than it is. But in spite of the testimony of Seth and many of his descendants, all men became corrupt. We read the record in Genesis 6 :1–7:

> And it came to pass, when men began to multiply on the face of the earth, and daughters were born unto them, That the sons of God saw the daughters of men that they were fair; and they took them wives of all which they chose. And the LORD said, My spirit shall not always strive with man, for that he also is flesh: yet his days shall be an hundred and twenty years. There were giants in the earth in those days; and also after that, when the sons of God came in unto the daughters of men, and they bare children to them, the same became mighty men which were of old, men of renown. And God saw that the wickedness of man was great in the earth, and that every imagination of the thoughts of his heart was only evil continually. And it repented the LORD that he had made man on the earth, and it grieved him at his heart. And the LORD said, I will destroy man whom I have created from the face of the earth; both man, and beast, and

the creeping thing, and the fowls of the air; for it repenteth me that I have made them.

Even under conditions of a twice cursed Earth, and the segregation of the lineage of Cain, man became more and more corrupt. The added dimension was the marrying of the "sons of God" with the "daughters of men." Sons of God in Scripture always refers to a direct creation of God. Subsequently, the whole human race, according to Moses, was "filled with violence through them."

The first identified civilization was Sumer. We read about Sumer from page 9 of *Wanderings* by Chaim Potok:

> What we see first when we gaze upon ancient Sumer in the year 3000 B.C.E. is a land about the size of Massachusetts or Belgium containing about a dozen cities, many of which are in plain view of one another. Dikes, ditches, and canals have been built to tame the waters of the two rivers and restrain the tide that comes from the Persian Gulf. . . . Civilization began with the cities of Sumer, Eridu, Ur, Erek, Lagash, Nippur, Kish, and others.

Sumer was located on a spot at the heart of the Garden of Eden. Archaeologists have not been able to identify to which racial division these people belong, because, as we believe, they were the descendants of Adam's sons when there was only one race. Sumer thrived between 3000 B.C. and 2400 B.C., placing this society before the Flood.

The inhabitants of the cities of Sumer kept detailed records and historical accounts on clay tablets. They wrote with wedge-shaped characters called cuneiform.

This first style of writing was adopted by the Assyrians, and many of the tablets left at Sumer were later copied by the Assyrians. In 1978 we visited the remains of the palace of King Ashurbanipal of Assyria where 25,000 cuneiform tablets were found.

Ancient Sumerian records reveal that city leaders were benevolent judges with little or no judicial authority. If crimes were committed they tried to get the people involved, and chaos resulted. There was constant war and violence. We quote C. Potok from page 11 of *Wanderings:*

> They try to practice mercy and compassion yet are more often than not motivated by an aggressive drive for prestige and success and show little consideration for the restraints of ethical behavior. The Sumerian lives in a world of constant fear. Above all, he fears the gods.

Some city dwellers worshipped as many as five hundred gods. These ancient accounts of the land of Sumer correspond with the description of the Antediluvians who lived on the other side of the Flood. But out of this violent, immoral, and corrupt civilization, God saw one man who believed in Him, and we read of this man in Genesis 6:8: "But Noah found grace in the eyes of the LORD."

Adam is called a son of God because he was created by God. After the fall of Adam, no son of God is named among the human race until Christ was born. The faithful who died before the cross went to paradise, also called Abraham's bosom, until Jesus died for their sins. Christians are sons of God by adoption through Jesus Christ, because they are born again of the Holy Spirit and created a new creature in Christ. Angels are called sons of God because they are also direct creations of God. But the meaning in the Hebrew for *sons of God* in Genesis 6:2 is "fallen ones," or fallen sons of God. Josephus said of this ungodly age before the Flood:

> Now this posterity of Seth continued to esteem God as the Lord of the universe, and to have an entire regard to virtue, for seven generations; but in process of time they were perverted, and forsook the practices of their forefathers, and did neither pay those honors to God which were appointed them, nor had they any concern to do justice towards men. But for what degree of zeal they had formerly shown for virtue, they now showed by their actions a double degree of wickedness; whereby they made God to be their enemy, for many angels of God accompanied with women, and begat sons that proved unjust, and despisers of all that was good, on account of the confidence they had in their own strength; for the tradition is, That these men did what resembled the acts of those whom the Grecians call giants.

Many believe that the sons of God of Genesis 6:2 were men from the lineage of Seth who married women from the lineage of Cain. However, a great host of Hebrew scholars contend that the text states plainly that they were fallen angels. Also, Philo, Tertullian, Justinian, Luther, Pember, and Wuest are just a few of the recognized scholars of the past who believe the scripture means that these were angels who left their "first estate" to follow Satan, and subsequently took women to be their wives (Jude 6). Jesus did say that the "angels of God in heaven" do not marry, but the qualification here is only to the angels who have remained faithful to God. Angels are always referred to as men in the Bible, and the perverts of Sodom sought to ravage the two angels who came to that city. Fallen angels came down to Earth because at that time all men, with the exception of Noah and a few others, had made God their enemy.

Noah was saved not because of anything that the patriarch had done, but rather because he believed God when He told him about the coming Flood. The result of God's grace is found in Hebrews 11:7:

> By faith Noah, being warned of God of things not seen as yet, moved with fear, prepared an ark to the saving of his house; by the which he condemned the world, and became heir of the righteousness which is by faith.

Out of the faith of Noah, God brought forth the nations from his sons, Ham, Shem, and Japheth.

Chapter 3

Babel and the
Post-Flood World

That there was a universal flood is beyond controversy. Concerning the Flood of Noah's day, which according to Scripture was to rid the earth of corrupted humanity, we quote from page 75 of *Halley's Bible Handbook:*

> Archives of the Temple of Marduk, in Babylon, as related by Berosus, 300 B.C., contained this story: Xisuthros, a king, was warned by one of the gods to build a ship, and take into it his friends and relatives and all different kinds of animals, with all necessary food. Whereupon he built an immense ship, which was stranded in Armenia. Upon subsidence of the Flood, he sent out birds; the third time, they returned not. He came out, builded an altar, and sacrificed. . . .
>
> Egyptians had a legend that the gods at one time purified the earth by a great Flood, from which only a few shepherds escaped.
>
> Greek tradition: Deucalion, warned that the gods were going to bring a flood upon the earth, for its great wickedness, built an ark, which rested on Mt. Parnassus. A dove was sent out twice.

Hindu tradition: Manu, warned, built a ship, in which he alone escaped from a Deluge which destroyed all creatures.

Chinese tradition: Fa-He, founder of Chinese civilization, is represented as having escaped from a Flood sent because man had rebelled against heaven and wife, 3 sons and 3 daughters.

England: Druids had a legend that the world had been re-peopled from a righteous patriarch who had been saved in a strong ship from a Flood sent to destroy man for his wickedness.

Polynesians have stories of a Flood from which 8 escaped.

Mexicans: One man, his wife and children, were saved in a ship from a Flood which overwhelmed the earth.

Peruvians: One man and one woman were saved in a box that floated on the flood waters.

American Indians: Various legends, in which 1, 3 or 8 persons were saved in a Boat above the waters on a high mountain.

Greenland: The earth once tilted over, and all men were drowned, except one man and one woman, who re-peopled the earth.

Babylonians, Assyrians, Egyptians, Persians, Hindus, Greeks, Chinese, Phrygians, Fiji Islanders, Esquimaux, Aboriginal Americans, Indians, Brazilians, Peruvians, and indeed every branch of the whole human race, Semitic, Aryan, Turanian—have traditions of a Great Deluge that destroyed all mankind, except one family, and which impressed itself indelibly on the memory of the ancestors of all these races before they separated. "All these myths are intelligible only on the supposition that some such event did actually occur. Such a universal belief, not springing from some instinctive principle of our nature, must be based on an Historical Fact."

From the book *Wanderings* by Chaim Potok, we read about the Sumerian account of the Flood on page 18:

> . . . One Sumerian tablet has been found thus far dealing with this ancient Deluge, and it is badly damaged. It tells us that the great gods . . . fashioned the black-headed people, vegetation, animals. They lowered kingship from heaven. . . . Then the gods talk of the Flood. . . . We are told that some of the gods wept over the coming devastation, and one of the gods took it upon himself to warn a pious king of the Deluge. The king built a boat. He sailed it seven days and seven nights as the tumultuous waters swept over the cult centers and the land. Then the storm ceased and the sun shone and the pious king opened a window of the boat and Utu, the sun god, shone his rays into the boat. . . . The king offered sacrifices to the gods. He was granted eternal life.

The similarity of these ancient accounts are sufficient to historically prove that there was a Flood that swept over the entire land mass of Earth—and a few souls were saved from a wicked generation to repopulate the earth. The Bible tells us that eight souls were saved: Noah and his wife; and Ham, Shem, and Japheth and their wives. If Ham, Shem, and Japheth had children at the time, they were probably old enough to make their own decisions to remain with that condemned generation (1 Pet. 3:20).

The ark of Noah came to rest on the mountain of Ararat, and Noah built an altar and offered clean animals as a sacrifice to God. We read in Genesis 8:21–22:

> And the LORD smelled a sweet savour; and the LORD
> said in his heart, I will not again curse the ground
> any more for man's sake; for the imagination of man's
> heart is evil from his youth; neither will I again smite
> any more every thing living, as I have done. While
> the earth remaineth, seedtime and harvest, and cold
> and heat, and summer and winter, and day and night
> shall not cease.

Before this time, man had not experienced extreme cold
or heat, summer or winter. This was part of the second
curse that God put on the creation because of the sins
of mankind. However, man had proven that his heart
was evil continually because of sin, and that he must
have a Redeemer to save him from sin. The sacrifice of
Noah looked forward to this Redeemer, the Lord Jesus
Christ, who would die for the sins of mankind. This was
the reason it rose as a sweet savour unto God. The Creator determined not to put another curse upon the earth,
and from the days of Noah to this time, the world, from
an environmental standpoint, has remained fairly stable.

We read of other changes that occurred after the
Flood in the eighth chapter of Genesis. Man felt wind
in his face for the first time, and in Genesis 9:13 it is related that Noah and his family saw a rainbow in the
clouds—this was the first time they had seen a rainbow.
We read of other changes in Genesis 9:1–6:

> And God blessed Noah and his sons, and said unto
> them, Be fruitful, and multiply, and replenish the
> earth. And the fear of you and the dread of you shall
> be upon every beast of the earth, and upon every

fowl of the air, upon all that moveth upon the earth, and upon all the fishes of the sea; into your hand are they delivered. Every moving thing that liveth shall be meat for you; even as the green herb have I given you all things. But flesh with the life thereof, which is the blood thereof, shall ye not eat. And surely your blood of your lives will I require; at the hand of every beast will I require it, and at the hand of man; at the hand of every man's brother will I require the life of man. Whoso sheddeth man's blood, by man shall his blood be shed: for in the image of God made he man.

God commanded the household of Noah to be fruitful—to have many sons and daughters, and replenish, or repopulate, the earth. However, man would now have more problems in repopulating the earth than he did before the Flood. He would no longer be able to communicate with the beasts of the earth [they would fear man], and many would rise up and attack him. Man was instructed to supplement his diet with animal flesh because the ground had been cursed a third time and the herbs and vegetables could not afford enough basic protein. Of course, we know today that eighty years is about as long as we can expect to live, even with the wonders of modern medicine and newly developed medical techniques. Also, women have quit bearing children at approximately forty-five years of age. If God had suddenly cut short man's life span it would have taken centuries and centuries for the earth to be repopulated, so the life span of man was shortened gradually. Noah lived to be 950 years of age; he lived for 350 years after the Flood. He died just fifty years before Abraham was born. It is entirely possible that Abraham saw one or more of Noah's three sons, Ham, Shem, and Japheth. Ham had thirty sons, Japheth had fourteen sons, and Shem had twenty-six sons. We are not told how many daughters they had. It certainly would be improbable for a woman to have this many children in a normal life span today. Peleg, who lived at the time of the Tower of Babel, lived to be 239 years of age, and Eber, a grandson of Noah, lived to 464 years of age. So even after the Flood, for about four hundred years, men lived to be several hundred years old, and had large families. This was for the purpose of the rapid replenishing of the earth with people, since God desired that all the earth be reinhabited again.

Concerning life after the Flood, we read that God told men they would be responsible for their own affairs. He instructed Noah and his sons that if a man willfully took the life of another man, the murderer's life (meaning manslayer) was to be taken from him in return. This commandment implied that a council of men would be responsible for administering justice and carrying out judgments. God did not permit man to exercise such responsibility before the Flood. He put a mark on Cain as a warning that men should not kill him. However, for the purpose of maintaining order in the world, and to give men the freedom to declare the truth of God so that others might be saved, God instituted human government. The rockbed of all such national, provincial, and local government is the law of capital punishment; the world would revert to the pre-Flood condition, and a similar judgment would have to be sent from God. Of course, in our day we have seen the abolishing of capital punishment in just about all nations, except the communist nations and the Moslem nations. Capital punishment was abolished in Venezuela in 1864;

Belgium in 1867; Argentina in 1921; Denmark in 1930; India in 1944; Finland in 1949; and Mexico in 1970. Even the Vatican City state abolished capital punishment in 1969. Few murderers in the U.S. have been executed since 1960, yet since that time the murder rate has doubled. From 1960 to 1972 alone the murder rate increased eighty percent.

The *1996 World Almanac* reported that in 1993 there were 2,716 prisoners on Death Row, yet in that year only thirty-eight were executed, and seventeen of these were in one state, Texas. Fifteen states as of 1993 did not have the death penalty, including heavily populated states like New York. Had these states had the death penalty, then the number on death row would have been closer to five thousand. Even in states that have the death penalty, it is practically impossible to carry out the execution, making it more probable that juries are reticent to access it. It is a sad commentary that in a nation where the Gospel is proclaimed more comprehensibly than in any other, the United States has the greatest percentage of the population in prison or on parole.

We could cite the records of fifty nations where capital punishment has been abolished, and the crime statistics have shown a steady increase. Before the Flood there was no capital punishment, and crime and violence filled the earth. Jesus said that "as it was in the days of Noah," so it would be when He came the second time.

After the Flood, God purposed to divide mankind into seventy nations from the descendants of the seventy grandsons of Noah. Subsequently, we will discuss these divisions according to race, nation, and language.

How men became different in color, spoke different languages, and developed different attitudes and skills according to their race, is one of the most interesting studies in the Bible, and it is often neglected. If everyone understood why we have different races, nations, and languages, there would be better understanding between men, and peace on Earth. Of course, the division of the human race into these many segments came because of sin. Before the Flood there was a population explosion because men and women were living to be almost a thousand years old. There would have been a minimum of six billion souls on Earth. There was no human government, with the exception of city societies, and sin abounded. The entire human race had become corrupt, and God had to destroy billions of people— everyone with the exception of Noah and his household. So, God determined to divide mankind thereafter into races, nations, and tongues. If a nation, like the Canaanite nation, became entirely corrupt (or a city, or a region like Sodom), then God could bring judgment upon the cancer without having to destroy all the races. Men in some nations could still come to the knowledge of the truth and be saved. God gave nations the opportunity to govern themselves, and when men do not uphold or cherish that consent from the Creator, then they fall under the heels of tyrants and oppressors. We find the reason God has divided mankind thus in 1 Timothy 2:1–6:

> I exhort therefore, that, first of all, supplications, prayers, intercessions, and giving of thanks, be made for all men; For kings, and for all that are in authority; that we may lead a quiet and peaceable life in all godliness and honesty. For this is good and acceptable in the sight of God our Saviour; Who will have all men to be saved, and to come unto the knowl-

edge of the truth. For there is one God, and one mediator between God and men, the man Christ Jesus; Who gave himself a ransom for all, to be testified in due time.

To this point in time after the Flood, God's purpose for the nations has been fulfilled. In spite of war, famine, pestilence and the ambitions of aspiring world dictators, there have been nations from which God's will for man has sprung. However, the time is coming when Satan will be successful for a period of seven years in bringing all nations under the authority of the Antichrist. Under the reign of the Devil's dictator, anyone who mentions the name of Jesus Christ will be killed.

For the present, Christians in the United States, just one of the nations that God has ordained, can be thankful that we have the freedom to declare the Gospel of Jesus Christ, even to the ends of the earth. Because of this we should pray for our governmental leaders every day.

Chapter 4

Ham, Shem, and Japheth

Before the Flood there were three outstanding witnesses for God in the world—Abel, Enoch, and Noah. These three are the only Antediluvian patriarchs mentioned in Hebrews 11. Seth was doubtless a righteous man, but his testimony did not compare with that of Abel, Enoch, or Noah. In these three witnesses for God, the pattern is established for all who are called according to the Lord's purpose. Abel was called to die for his faith, and all down through the ages, in every dispensation, some are called to lay their bodies on the altar as a living sacrifice, even unto death. Enoch was translated for his faith. He was called out of the world that would come under judgment. In every age, some are called out according to their faith. Abraham was called out of Ur; Lot was called out of Sodom; Israel was called out of Egypt; and Christians will be called out of the world before the Tribulation falls. Noah also walked with God in faith, but he was not called to die or to be translated. He was called to occupy, and occupy he did. Enoch is a type of the church to be taken out of the world before the·"man of sin" is revealed. Noah is a type of Israel, the 144,000 witnesses of God, who will be called to witness in a world that is totally corrupted.

In Genesis 9:18–29 we read of the men from which the different races would come after the Flood:

> And the sons of Noah, that went forth of the ark, were Shem, and Ham, and Japheth: and Ham is the father of Canaan. These are the three sons of Noah: and of them was the whole earth overspread. And Noah began to be an husbandman, and he planted a vineyard: And he drank of the wine, and was drunken; and he was uncovered within his tent. And Ham, the father of Canaan, saw the nakedness of his father, and told his two brethren without. And Shem and Japheth took a garment, and laid it upon both their shoulders, and went backward, and covered the nakedness of their father; and their faces were backward, and they saw not their father's nakedness. And Noah awoke from his wine, and knew what his younger son had done unto him. And he said, Cursed be Canaan; a servant of servants shall he be unto his brethren. And he said, Blessed be the LORD God of Shem; and Canaan shall be his servant. God shall enlarge Japheth, and he shall dwell in the tents of Shem; and Canaan shall be his servant. And Noah lived after the flood three hundred and fifty years. And all the days of Noah were nine hundred and fifty years: and he died.

Of the seventy grandsons of Noah mentioned in Scripture, Canaan is selected for special mention. In Genesis 9:18 none of the sons of Shem and Japheth are noted, but we are told that Ham is the father of Canaan. Of course, we read quite plainly in the Bible that only eight souls were saved from the Flood. It is fairly certain that the eight souls were Noah, Mrs. Noah, and Ham, Shem, and Japheth, and their three wives. It might be concluded from verse 18 of Genesis 9 that Canaan was born in the ark, except for the fact that Genesis 10:6 indicates that Canaan was the fifth son of Ham, and there were probably several daughters born along with the first five sons. Therefore, the only reason we can gather for the special mention of Canaan is that it was upon him that the curse of Noah fell, and God wanted us to be sure to keep our eye on this man.

So Noah settled down with his wife and three sons at the lower levels on Mt. Ararat. At the foot of Mt. Ararat today is a town called Naxuana, which means, "Noah settled here," or became a husbandman here. And Noah planted a vineyard. The area at Naxuana is still good for growing grapes, and the natives in this region claim they can still locate the place where Noah planted and cultivated his grape orchard. From the grapes, Noah made wine. This is the first time that wine, or any alcoholic beverage, is mentioned in Scripture. Wine, or alcohol, is made from the fermenting action produced by microbes. It may not have been possible to produce alcohol before the Flood. It is entirely possible that Noah put some sugar, or some other sweetening agent, into his grape juice. After a few days it began to ferment, and Noah may have gotten drunk quite by accident. We don't know for sure that this is the way it happened, but it is entirely possible.

After the Flood, the life span of man began to decline as declared in Genesis 6:3:

> And the LORD said, My spirit shall not always strive with man, for that he also is flesh: yet his days shall be an hundred and twenty years.

The age expectancy of man gradually declined until it reached threescore and ten years as established in the

Scriptures. But God said that man's days would never exceed 120 years in the ages to come. The 1974 edition of the *Guinness Book of World Records* states that there is no evidence, in spite of several claims, that any man or woman in secular history (apart from the Bible record of the Antediluvians), has ever lived to be more than 120 years of age. A few have reached this age, but none have surpassed it.

As Noah lay naked in his tent, the Scripture declares that Ham saw him. The terminology used may imply more than just seeing with the eyes. For example, the Bible uses the verb "knew" to explain the act of conception.

Before the Flood, sexual perversion was rampant. The terminology used in Genesis 6:5–6,12 to describe the condition of mankind was:

> . . . the wickedness of man was great in the earth . . . every imagination of the thoughts of his heart was only evil continually. And it repented the LORD that he had made man on the earth, and it grieved him at his heart. . . . God looked upon the earth, and, behold, it was corrupt; for all flesh had corrupted his way upon the earth.

In all probability the Apostle Paul was referring to the destruction of the Antediluvians when he wrote in Romans 1:26–27:

> For this cause God gave them up unto vile affections: for even their women did change the natural use into that which is against nature: And likewise also the men, leaving the natural use of the woman, burned in their lust one toward another; men with men working that which is unseemly. . .

God did not create men and women to be sexually perverted. This condition developed afterward, and it would appear from the entire text of Scripture that it resulted from the union of fallen angels with women. We read of the fallen angels and their association with sexual perversion in Jude 6–7:

> And the angels which kept not their first estate, but left their own habitation, he hath reserved in everlasting chains under darkness unto the judgment of the great day. Even as Sodom and Gomorrah, and the cities about them in like manner, giving themselves over to fornication, and going after strange flesh . . .

We note the specific wording of Genesis 9:24: "And Noah awoke from his wine, and knew what his younger son had done unto him." It would certainly appear that there was more involved here than Ham just stumbling by chance upon the drunken body of his father. We read in Genesis 6:9 that Noah was "perfect in his generations." Noah was not perfect in that he was sinless, he was perfect in that he escaped the corruption that had affected all flesh. However, nothing is said about Noah's wife, or the wives of Ham, Shem, or Japeth, so a genetic flaw may have been passed on to Ham and Canaan through Mrs. Noah.

Canaan seemed to have been involved in the sin of Ham. He could have been with his father and a participant in the deed, or while Ham was gone to tell his brothers about their father's condition, Canaan could have become equally guilty. We readily admit that our explanation of what possibly happened is conjecture; however, God would not have extended the curse to

Canaan had he been only an innocent bystander. It is no wonder that Noah was upset because one of the sins that brought about the judgment of the pre-Flood society had now appeared in his own household. There is a Jewish interpretation that Noah's nakedness could be a reference to Noah's wife, and Canaan was the result of an incestuous relationship.

Because of the deed of Ham, and the response to that act by his two brothers, the time had come for Noah to establish the order of God's blessing in the dividing of the nations. Again, we see the part that sin played in the segregation of mankind into races, languages, and tongues.

In the genealogy of nations from the three sons of Noah given in Genesis 10, the noted Hebrew scholar Dr. A. Cohen makes the following comment on page 48 of *The Books of the Bible:*

> The sons of Japheth. He is mentioned first, because he was the eldest. Then follows Ham, the youngest, so that the genealogy of Shem, leading to Abraham, can be given without break.

Japheth, being the eldest, was due the primary blessing, and Shem a secondary blessing. The initial blessing of God, under the Old Testament economy, beginning with Cain, passed to the eldest son. God told Cain that he would rule over Abel—he would have the faith of Abel—but Cain did not, and he lost the blessing.

Shem being the second son in Noah's household received a conditional blessing. We read in Genesis 9:26, "And he said, Blessed be the LORD God of Shem. . . ." The blessing was not on Shem, but on the Lord God of Shem—the Messiah, the Christ, in whom all the world would be blessed. Shem would be blessed as long as he and his descendants placed their faith in the Lord God. This is why, throughout the Old Testament, in at least fifty commandments, the descendants of Shem are admonished not to forget the Lord their God, because if they forgot Him, the blessing of God through Noah would depart from them. We read in Deuteronomy 8:11, "Beware that thou forget not the LORD thy God. . . ." And over and over in Ezekiel, Jeremiah, Amos, and many of the other prophets, it is prophesied that because Israel would forget the Lord their God, they would be pillaged, their women raped, their houses burned, and they would be scattered into all the nations of the world—and they would not be gathered back until the Messiah comes to judge the nations.

In our chart on the nations, we have traced for you the countries, races, and languages which came from Shem. As long as the mainstream of the Shemitic peoples, the descendants of Abraham, honored God and kept His commandments, all Shemitic peoples received a secondary blessing. These peoples included the Arabic countries and the nations in the Orient. We can go back in history to the time when Israel was at its height under David and Solomon, and find that the great dynasties in China were likewise at the pinnacle of cultural and economic development. The ruins of great cities that once thrived during this age can be found in the jungles of Cambodia, Thailand, and Burma. During this time the Hamitic peoples, for the most part, were either living in an uncivilized state or, like the Canaanite tribes, living in immorality and idolatry. The descendants of Canaan settled Sodom, Gomorrah, and the cities thereabouts. They inherited the curse upon Ham through Canaan, and they became a sexually perverted society, and God destroyed them. Later, when the Israelites came into the land of Canaan, God commanded that all the Canaanites, including the little children, be destroyed. Atheists and agnostics have picked upon this edict of God to try to discredit the Bible, but there was a reason for God to give this commandment. Excavations of the ancient Canaanite cities reveal that these people were idol worshippers and they sacrificed babies to their gods. Also, medical studies of their bones show that even the infants were born with venereal disease.

The name *Shem* means "renown," but when the line of God's blessings to the Shemitic people, the Hebrews, forgot the Lord their God, the blessing was removed, and the entire race—from the Chinese, to the Hindus, to the Israelites, declined. The descendants of Ham settled the continent of Africa. The most noted accomplishment of any of the Hamitic nations was the Egyptian Empire.

Chapter 5

The Times of the Gentiles

In Genesis 10 the national line of descent begins with Japheth, the eldest. After the birth record of the fourteenth and last son of Japheth, we read in verse 5: "By these were the isles of the Gentiles divided in their lands."

The Hebrew word for "Gentile" is *goyim,* and most commentaries today interpret the word to mean all races apart from the Hebrew race, and all nations other than Israel. However, some words have changed in meaning over the centuries. The word *Jew* first appeared during the Babylonian captivity, and it applied to the captives, the vast majority of whom were from the tribe of Judah. Later, the term *Jew* meant any Israelite.

In the initial sense, the primary blessing of Noah went to the descendants of Japheth, called *Gentiles* in Genesis 5. Later, especially in the New Testament, the term *Gentile* was further qualified in meaning to refer to every other race, religion, nation, and tongue apart from the descendants of Isaac. First, Gentiles referred to the descendants of Japheth; second, to all nations and races apart from the lineage of Shem; and finally, to all people on Earth with the exception of the descendants of Isaac. Jesus said in reference to Gentiles in Luke 21:24:

> And they [meaning Israel] shall fall by the edge of
> the sword, and shall be led away captive into all na-
> tions: and Jerusalem shall be trodden down of the
> Gentiles, until the times of the Gentiles be fulfilled.

The times of the Gentiles began with the treading down of Jerusalem by Babylon in about 600 B.C. Babylon was an outgrowth of Babel. The city was ruled by Nimrod, a descendant of Ham, and for this reason many think that Babel was racially Hamitic. After the races were separated into nations and tongues, Babylon became predominantly Shemitic. Between Babel and Babylon there arose two other great empires—Egypt, which was Hamitic, and Assyria, which was Shemitic. No great identifiable Japhetic nation, empire, or society had appeared up to the time that Nebuchadnezzar destroyed Jerusalem.

The blessing of Noah (the patriarchal head of all nations) upon Shem was predicated, as we have already pointed out, upon the Lord God. This blessing was passed on to Abraham, and then Isaac. When the recipients of the blessing forgot the Lord their God, the ten northern tribes were taken captive by Assyria, and one hundred years later the two southern tribes went into captivity in Babylon. From the treading down of Jerusalem in 607 B.C., the times of the Gentiles began, and no major Hamitic or Shemitic nation or empire arose until the last days. Japheth dwelt in the tents of Shem and, as a result, the time of his enlargement began.

A Japhetic alliance, Medo-Persia, defeated Babylon in 538 B.C. and became the world's dominant empire. The conquest of the Persian Empire was completed by Alexander in 323 B.C. Greece, another Japhetic empire, replaced Persia as the ruler of the known and recognized world at that time. The Grecian Empire was divided into four parts, and as a result gradually weakened. Rome, also a Japhetic empire, rose up to the west and moved into the Middle East to fill the vacuum. The breakup of the Roman Empire occurred over a five hundred-year period, from about A.D. 500 to A.D. 1000. It broke up into national identities, or as explained in Daniel 2, "big chunks." It was in this broken state that Rome continued to rule the world through a succession of European Japhetic empires: the Spanish Empire, the French Empire, the German Empire, the Dutch Empire, the Belgian Empire, the British Empire, etc. The slogan that "the sun never set on the British Empire" could also apply to the others. In a subsequent study we will discuss in greater detail how the breakup of the Japhetic empires was accomplished after World War II and how it fits into Bible prophecy.

The main point we wish to stress at this time is that the times of the Gentiles is in accordance with the primary blessing given to Japheth by Noah, and the reason that the great empires which have risen and fallen since 600 B.C. were Japhetic. Of course, there are a few minor exceptions, but even these do not interrupt the flow of prophecy from the days of Nebuchadnezzar to this very hour. In about A.D. 600 the Mohammedan religion flourished under the leadership of Mohammed, and much of the Middle East from Turkey to Egypt was taken and held for a time. The Moors invaded Italy and southern Spain, but this was a temporary religious condition that in no way threatened the Japhetic empires and their hold upon the world. In the third and fourth century the Byzantine Empire flourished, but this empire was actually the eastern half of the Roman Empire which had been granted autonomy for economic and military reasons. The capital of the Byzantine Empire was Constantinople, a Japhetic and European city.

There is another reference to the Gentiles in Romans 11:25–28:

> For I would not, brethren, that ye should be ignorant of this mystery, lest ye should be wise in your own conceits; that blindness in part is happened to Israel, until the fulness of the Gentiles be come in. And so all Israel shall be saved: as it is written, There shall come out of Sion the Deliverer, and shall turn away ungodliness from Jacob: For this is my covenant unto them, when I shall take away their sins. As concerning the gospel, they are enemies for your sakes: but as touching the election, they are beloved for the fathers' sakes.

The reference in the preceding scripture states that in relation to the Gospel of Jesus Christ, there was blindness in Israel. Some, like Paul, believe that Jesus Christ was the Messiah who died on the cross for sin; He was buried, and rose again the third day. However, the majority in Israel did not accept Jesus as the promised Deliverer and Redeemer, but Paul wrote to the Romans that when the "fulness of the Gentiles" occurred, then Jesus Christ would come back to Israel as the great Deliverer and take away their sins. The word *fullness* could also be interpreted "enlargement," or "the completed enlargement." In this sense, the "fulness of the Gentiles" and the "times of the Gentiles" parallel each other. However, the times of the Gentiles is associated with the treading down of Jerusalem, or nationalistic Gentile military power, while the "fulness of the Gentiles" is related to the Gospel of Jesus Christ, and the rejection by

Israel of the Gospel until this future event occurs. The fullness of the Gentiles can also be understood in light of the statement by James in Acts 15:14–16:

> Simeon hath declared how God at the first did visit the Gentiles, to take out of them a people for his name. And to this agree the words of the prophets; as it is written, After this I will return, and will build again the tabernacle of David, which is fallen down; and I will build again the ruins thereof, and I will set it up.

Therefore, the fullness of the Gentiles, as many believe, encompasses the great number during the dispensation of grace who have been saved, or will be saved, by the preaching of the Gospel of Jesus Christ. There is reason to believe that there is a definite number of souls established by God to be saved in the Church Age. It has also been suggested that inasmuch as the church is to reign with Jesus Christ in "heavenly places" (Eph. 1–2), then we will inherit those heavenly principalities that are now occupied by the fallen angels. It is prophesied in Revelation 12:7–9:

> And there was war in heaven: Michael and his angels fought against the dragon; and the dragon fought and his angels, And prevailed not; neither was their place found any more in heaven. And the great dragon was cast out, that old serpent, called the Devil, and Satan, which deceiveth the whole world: he was cast out into the earth, and his angels were cast out with him.

We do not say in all certainty that the completed number of Christ's church will be the same as the angels of the Devil who will be cast out of heaven, but this is an interesting thought, and a very possible one. In any event, there is a preordained number of men, women, and children to be saved in the Church Age. Peter said this body would be taken from among the Gentiles. Luke recorded Paul as saying in Acts 28:27–28:

> For the heart of this people is waxed gross, and their ears are dull of hearing, and their eyes have they closed; lest they should see with their eyes, and hear with their ears, and understand with their heart, and should be converted, and I should heal them. Be it known therefore unto you, that the salvation of God is sent unto the Gentiles, and that they will hear it.

When the Apostle Paul, God's apostle to the Gentiles, was in Asia Minor, he had a vision from the Lord as recorded in Acts 16:8–10:

> And they passing by Mysia came down to Troas. And a vision appeared to Paul in the night; There stood a man of Macedonia, and prayed him, saying, Come over into Macedonia, and help us. And after he had seen the vision, immediately we endeavoured to go into Macedonia, assuredly gathering that the Lord had called us for to preach the gospel unto them.

The Holy Spirit revealed to Paul that he was not to go farther into Asia Minor, then the vision appeared of a man in Macedonia asking him to come westward with the Gospel. In his epistles Paul does not mention any calling or desire to go eastward to Syria or Babylon with the Gospel, but he often mentioned his yearnings to go to Rome and to Spain. So the Gospel of Jesus Christ that was to be preached to the Gentiles went westward to the Japhetic nations. Paul wrote to the church at Ephesus in Ephesians 3:1–2:

> For this cause I Paul, the prisoner of Jesus Christ for you Gentiles, If ye have heard of the dispensation of the grace of God which is given me to you-ward.

From the first century to the nineteenth century, the nations that received the Gospel of Jesus Christ and established churches were predominantly the Japhetic nations. This is a fact of history. The Shemitic nations and Hamitic nations for the most part remained under the influence of Buddhism, Hinduism, Shintoism, Mohammedism, or voodooism, and in this light of history, it is apparent that when Paul said that the Gentiles would hear the Gospel and receive it, he was referring mainly to the Japhetic race. During the Church Age some Jews have believed the Gospel and been saved. People of the black, yellow, and brown races have likewise heard the Gospel and been added to the body of Christ. However, for the most part, it has been the descendants of Japheth who have embraced the Gospel and sent missionaries to other peoples of the world.

The blessing upon Japheth was twofold: He would dwell in the tents of Shem, and he would be enlarged. Japheth and his descendants would be blessed both materially and spiritually. This has been fulfilled during the times of the Gentiles, but we would be careful to point out that concerning the spiritual blessing given to Japheth for the Church Age, this does not mean that God has ordained members of one race to be saved and those of another race to be lost. The Gospel invitation is given in John 3:16:

For God so loved the world, that he gave his only begotten Son, that whosoever believeth in him should not perish, but have everlasting life.

In the eighth chapter of Acts the conversation of the Ethiopian eunuch is recorded. According to tradition, he returned to Ethiopia and founded the Coptic Church there. The Ethiopian Coptic Church is the oldest known Christian church in existence, and this is doubtless the reason that Ethiopia has remained, for the most part, an independent national entity during the Japhetic colonial age.

As far as the descendants of Ham are concerned, during the times of the Gentiles until the nineteenth century, the majority were segregated by the Sahara desert and the jungles of Africa, where even the gold-hungry armies of Spain were fearful of venturing. A position of servitude assigned to the descendants of Ham has been verified during the enlargement of Japheth. In 1619, Negro slaves were landed at Jamestown by the Dutch, and slavery became common in the North American English colonies. In 1650, chattel slavery was legalized. The Civil War that came two hundred years later to abolish slavery is a matter of history.

However, Jesus said that when Jerusalem would no longer be "trodden down of the Gentiles" the times of the Gentiles would come to an end. The times of the Gentiles began to wind down after World War II. The Japhetic empires began to break up. The Dutch gave up the long string of Pacific islands now known as Indonesia; England gave up India and colonies in the Far East; France, Belgium, and Portugal gave up the Hamitic nations of Africa. The stage was being set for the fulfillment of the prophecy in Luke 21:24:

> And they shall fall by the edge of the sword, and shall
> be led away captive into all nations: and Jerusalem
> shall be trodden down of the Gentiles, until the times
> of the Gentiles be fulfilled.

The Jews began returning to the land and Israel became a nation on schedule as the Japhetic empires began to break up. The times of the Gentiles has come to an end. The world is in a transition period at this time waiting for the "fulness of the Gentiles" to be completed.

Paul wrote in Colossians 3:11 that in Christ, "there is neither Greek nor Jew, circumcision nor uncircumcision, Barbarian, Scythian, bond nor free: but Christ is all, and in all."

There are millions of people of every race that make up the church, the body of Christ, but this truth in no way negates another truth—that both the spiritual and material blessings that God through Noah gave to Japheth have been fulfilled with the time spans of the times of the Gentiles and the "fulness of the Gentiles."

What the nations have to look forward to is a time of trouble such as the world has never seen (Matt. 24:21), but after the hold of Satan upon the nations of this planet has been broken at the battle of Armageddon, then all wars and injustices that exist between the countries of the world will be resolved. Then the descendants of all three of Noah's sons will dwell in the tents of Jesus Christ.

> And it shall come to pass, that every one that is left
> of all the nations which came against Jerusalem shall
> even go up from year to year to worship the King,
> the LORD of hosts, and to keep the feast of tabernacles.
> —Zechariah 14:16

Chapter 6

World Languages

The most reliable history book in the world is the Bible. Its accurate and unbiased presentation of man's origin and development on planet Earth is God's perfect record of man's humble origin in the Garden of Eden. Then it proceeds to describe how the first human couple began to reproduce until there were millions of human beings. It vividly tells how the human family began to spread across the surface of the globe.

As the population multiplied into hundreds and millions there was one spoken language by which these people communicated with each other. This single language persisted beyond the Flood, until the great city of Babel was erected. We read the biblical commentary on this: "And the whole earth was of one language, and of one speech" (Gen. 11:1).

That original single language of pre-Babel days was proto-Hebrew, the language of Adam and Eve, and their children. It was the language evidently taught to Adam by God and became the medium of communication between them. It was basically the same language used by God in His communications with Abraham the patriarch, with Moses the prophet on Mount Sinai, and with Paul the apostle on the Damascus Road. It is the language that will be the principal mode of written and spoken communications during the Millennium.

Now with such a beautiful language designed by God for man's daily use, we ask ourselves, why was it necessary to break up the language into many new divisions? This prevented a man speaking one language from understanding someone speaking another language, or dialect. Genesis 11 chronicles for us the reason God broke up one language into many languages. Genesis 10 tells us that after the Flood (about 2400 B.C.), the whole population of the world stemmed from the three sons of Noah—Shem, Ham, and Japheth. Genesis 10 names twenty-six nations that sprang from the loins of Shem. Thirty nations came from Ham, and fourteen nations descended from Japheth, totaling seventy nations in all. These nations instead of speaking the single proto-Hebrew of Antediluvian times now began to speak in other tongues. We read in Genesis 11:7–8 how God interposed His sovereign will upon the human race at that critical juncture in history. We discover His purpose for that Divine intervention:

> Go to, let us go down, and there confound their language, that they may not understand one another's speech. So the LORD scattered them abroad from thence upon the face of all the earth. . . .

Genesis 11 explains that the cause of this Divine correction of the course plotted by the human politician/navigators of that day, was their apostasy. They turned away from worshipping God. The descendants of Ham, one of Noah's sons, were led by "a mighty hunter [Nimrod . . .] And the beginning of his kingdom was Babel" (Gen. 10:9–10).

God's ideal for humanity was mankind to be "one," united by one universal language. That ideal, of course, will be largely restored in the coming Millennium, but not before. Because of the pernicious rebellion of man against God, humanity was now divided, by Divine decree, by the diversity of languages. The differences in languages has since become a source of considerable misunderstanding, hostility, and war. Man is still trying to build himself another Babel. When God intervened in the building of the first skyscraper, the Tower of Babel, the builders

> ... left off to build the city. Therefore is the name of it called Babel [or confusion]; because the LORD did there confound the language of all the earth: and from thence did the LORD scatter them abroad upon the face of all the earth
> —Genesis 11 :8–9

Thus, the original divinely-ordained unity of language which was necessary for the unity of mankind was lost at Babel. A grave transgression was committed by Nimrod and his associates, so it is not surprising that their insolence provoked Divine punishment.

Today, in the twentieth century, the original seventy national languages that emerged at Babel have now proliferated into over three thousand known tongues spoken around the globe! God has certainly shown His fierce disapproval of Nimrod's new post-Flood civilization, and three thousand modern languages amply testify to the lasting nature of God's retribution. Every time we hear a foreign tongue spoken we are reminded that the one single cause of such diversity of languages goes back directly to the revolt at the Tower of Babel.

The three main branches of the world's languages are tied up with the three sons of Noah. Generally speaking, Asia was given to Shem, Africa to Ham, and Europe to Japheth. In the same general manner, scholars have traced all existing languages to three original sources. These three sources in turn are derived from a primeval spring which we call proto-Hebrew. The more we examine the allotment of Europe, Asia, and Africa among the three sons of Noah, the more vividly we see the remarkable fulfillment of prophecy referring to them. In running down the catalog of nations in Genesis 10, there is little difficulty in recognizing them. As we recognize the nations, we can trace the languages that characterize them.

The Semitic Languages

Shem is singled out in Genesis 10:21. Shem is called "the father of all the children of Eber" (from which Hebrew is derived). In Eber the main line divided into that of Peleg, from whom the lineage of Abraham and the descendants of Joktan sprang. The descendants of Shem are practically, and almost exclusively, Asiatic nations. A few of these basic Asiatic peoples, or Semites, migrated to other areas. For instance, the Amerindians, as we know them in North America, Central America, and South America, are not Japhetic, but Semitic in origin. These tribes today are not as numerous as they once were, but they are still visible and indigenous. Since A.D. 70 the Semitic Jews, whose country, Israel, is in Asia, were scattered across the world in what is called the Diaspora or "dispersion." Today there are more Jews in North America than in Israel. However, they are not Japhetic, but clearly Semitic. This applies to their language, Hebrew, which is likewise a Semitic language.

Arabic, is also a Semitic language and is spoken by Israel's Arab neighbors. Furthermore, Aramaic, the language used in Palestine after the Babylonian captivity (606–536 B.C.), and spoken by Jesus and His disciples, was in a group of northwest Semitic languages spoken in biblical times. However, the Semitic languages are not by any means confined to the Middle East. When you push all the way over to the Pacific Ocean, you discover that there are about one billion people today who speak some form of the basic Mandarin Chinese.

Many Hebrew words used today have precisely the same meaning as when they were first reduced to writing in Abraham's day, or even earlier in Adam's day. That is why the Bible is such a fascinating book. We are reading the very words appointed by the Holy Spirit, and then breathed into the minds and memories of first the Antediluvian patriarchs, and then into the minds of prophets in later centuries. It is only right that Hebrew should be the language *par excellence*. After all, Israel is at the crossroads of the world. It is the bridge between the three vast continents of Europe, Africa, and Asia. It, therefore, should have caught no one by surprise when, in 1980, it became the official language of the new republic of Israel. It is the most ancient language of the world, and it is being used today as the most modern. It has outlived every other language known to man.

Another highly intriguing aspect of this Semitic branch of world languages is that it is not only the language used by both God and man, but it is also a language in which angels were conversant. For instance:

> And the angel of the LORD called unto Abraham out of heaven the second time, And said, By myself have I sworn, saith the LORD, for because thou hast done

this thing, and hast not withheld thy son, thine only son: That in blessing I will bless thee . . . because thou hast obeyed my voice.

—Genesis 22:15–18

In an earlier account Abraham had a regular dialogue with angels, who appeared as men at his tent door. They even asked him in Hebrew where his wife Sarah was, and he told them that she was in the tent (Gen. 18:2,9). So here then is one of the three thousand languages of planet Earth that was spoken by God, spoken by angels, and spoken by man.

Further, this unique Semitic language was not only utilized as a direct means of communication from the dawn of human history, in pre-Flood days, in New Testament times, and today, but it is the language of the future. We read in Zephaniah 3:8–9:

> Therefore wait ye upon me, saith the LORD, until the day that I rise up to the prey: for my determination is to gather the nations, that I may assemble the kingdoms, to pour upon them mine indignation, even all my fierce anger: for all the earth shall be devoured with the fire of my jealousy. For then will I turn to the people [that is the peoples, the nations, the Gentiles] a pure language, that they may all call upon the name of the LORD, to serve him with one consent.

This terminology obviously means the last days when a remnant of Israel has returned to the land, and in the day of preparation for the battle of Armageddon. In 1980 Eleazier Ben Yehuda got a law passed in the Knesset to again make Hebrew the official language of Israel. In 1991 Israel flew fifteen thousand black Falasha Jews out of Ethiopia to Tel Aviv in one weekend, and as noted, even these would have to learn to speak Hebrew. All this has come to pass in Israel already, but this may also have a reference to the Millennium when the entire world as one will speak Hebrew in the universal government of Jesus Christ.

We have already examined the dominant features of the Semitic branch of languages. Now let us view the Hamitic and Japhetic language segments.

Hamitic Languages

The Hamitic branch of the human language family represents the thirty nations that sprang from the loins of Ham. Ham's descendants mostly migrated to Africa, just as Shem's offspring settled in Asia. The Hamitic branch of languages is largely confined today to Africa, and none of them can be considered universal. Few, if any, of the present-day Hamitic languages are spoken by more than 30 million people. In the case of the Semitic languages, many of them are spoken by hundreds of millions. There are at least thirteen Semitic languages, each of which is spoken by well over 30 million people. Non-Africans are sometimes prone to think of Africans as largely speaking one broad African language. However, nothing could be further from the truth. Of the three races that sprang from the three sons of Noah, the Hamitic stream had the largest number of nations listed in the roster of nations found in Genesis 10. The Japhetic stream that largely settled in Europe had only fourteen nations listed. The Semitic branch that migrated all over Asia claimed twenty-six nations.

In considering the Hamitic language we must realize that the Hamitic peoples represented the earliest imperial world power, first under Nimrod in Babylonia (Asia), and later in such ancient empires as Ashur and

Nineveh on the upper Tigris. Further, Egypt, which was founded by these same people, became a powerful centralized authority.

The Hamitic languages are of considerable interest to Americans because of Christian missionary work conducted in Africa. The American Bible Society, the British and Foreign Bible Society, and of late, the Wycliffe Bible Translators, have all sought to reduce the many spoken languages and dialects in Africa into written form so that Bibles could be read by the modern Hamitic peoples. In Ethiopia, the predominant religion is a form of Christianity called *Coptic,* and the official language spoken today is not Ethiopic but Amharic, a southern Semitic language. In Zaire (formerly Belgian Congo), a country of 24 million people, Bible societies have many problems in language. According to latest reports, translations of the Bible into local languages or dialects are still being made. The United Bible Societies report that for the first time there is now "a New Testament in Kituba; Mark's Gospel in Bangala, Izaka, and Kisuku; John's Gospel in Kinandi; Romans in Chokwe; Luke 15 in Iyansi, Kinandi, Kisongye, Lingombe, Swahili, Tshiluba." You can readily see the formidable task there is today in communicating the Bible to all the Hamitic tribes, nations, and races, because of the many dialects that have to be mastered by Christian missionaries working in the land of Ham.

Japhetic Languages

Last of all, we make a brief survey of the Japhetic languages. We are more familiar with these. We may even, in the course of high school or college education, have studied one or more of the Japhetc languages as we know them today. The Japhetic branch of languages is linked with Japheth, a son of Noah. Japheth, according to the table of nations in Genesis 10, gave rise to fourteen nations, one or more of which most Americans have an organic bond. If our forebears came from Europe, then almost certainly we have a Japhetic heritage, culture, and language. Of all the Japhetic languages, there are at least twelve spoken by more than 30 million people each. The principal language of the United States is English, which goes back to Anglo-Saxon roots. The British are a very mixed people, having entertained successive invasions from Vikings, Romans, Normans, and other continental peoples, all of whom left their mark by intermarriage with the original inhabitants, and made their impact on the language as well as the culture. For instance, the name of the capital city of Great Britain, London, derived from the Roman name *Londinium*. If your forebears were Scots/Irish, then they were Celts, and the original language was Celtic, spoken by the Bretons, Irish, Welsh, and Highland Scots.

Also, in the field of language, the Japhetic peoples demonstrated their ability to impose their languages on other peoples. Not many people outside of Africa speak Hamitic languages. Likewise, not many people outside of Asia speak Semitic languages. However, the marked exception is to be found among Japhetic or enlarged nations. French, Portuguese, Spanish, and most conspicuously English, are not only spoken in the lands of Japheth—Europe—but they are spoken in North and South America, and all over Asia, and Africa.

Even in the case of the Jews who belong to the Semitic (or Shemitic) family, Hebrew is not spoken by peoples other than Hebrews. However, when the Bible came to the Japhetic peoples of the western world, they did more to propagate the knowledge of God as revealed in His Holy Word than all of the Hamitic and Semitic peoples put together. It was the enlarged Japhetic people who have been the principal missionaries, who have not only proclaimed God's Word to Asia, Africa, and the rest of the world, but who have taken on the tedious task of translating the Hebrew/Greek Bible into the tongues of well over a thousand different languages. They have been the pioneers in taking what was basically a Semitic book and making certain that all three branches of the human family would have access to its fabulous treasures. The Bible is a best-seller of books because the Japhetic peoples made sure that the enlarging characteristics bestowed upon them would include the spreading of God's Word to all the nations. The Japhetic peoples have not only enlarged geographically, but space-exploration-wise, language-wise, and most importantly, in the spiritual realm. They have been the greatest missionaries to "go . . . and teach all nations" by means of the written and spoken Word. William Carey in India, Hudson Taylor in China, and David Livingstone in Africa, blazed the trails into the lands of Shem and Ham to communicate the Gospel in a language known to the nationals of those distant lands. It is a romantic and glorious chapter that has preceded the end of the Church Age.

In addition to the laborious translation of the living Word into thousands of tongues, a process occupying years of tedious linguistic activity, the Japhetic peoples have brought a still added dimension to the language proclamation of Christ in our day. The Japhetic nations invented the modern printing press which enabled us to mass produce Bibles. However, now with radio and television, the horizons of Christian witness have been enlarged even further. America is at the forefront of such activity, and today God's Word is being proclaimed in more languages than at any time in human history.

What a colossal responsibility, what a superb opportunity, is presented to the United States to use the medium of language to proclaim the unsearchable riches of Christ to the final generation of the Church Age before it closes forever and the Church is raptured, and the Gospel broadcasting facilities are curtailed or muzzled. We must not fail. We have the technical means of reaching more millions by radio and television than any generation preceding us. God holds us accountable to reach the far corners of the globe with the saving message of the risen and soon-coming Christ.

Chapter 7

End-Time Alignment of Nations

It is evident that we are living in the terminal generation of the Church Age. The Church Age is an epoch
that immediately precedes a seven-year period known
as "Daniel's seventieth week." This "week of years" is
called elsewhere the "Great Tribulation" and the "time
of Jacob's trouble" in Scripture. It is of vivid interest to
Bible students how the basic seventy nations of Genesis
10–11 will finally align in these last days.

Three Racial Streams
The three racial streams that found their source in Noah,
have across over four millennia spread out to cover the
globe. The bulk of Japheth's descendants moved after
the Flood in a western direction and settled in Europe.
They had actually migrated from the landing arena of
Noah's Ark which rested on Mount Ararat, in Turkey, to
Europe. In the Church Age, they pushed on westward
to North America, Australia, and New Zealand. Today,
the European Community of fifteen basic nations
roughly occupy territory formerly within the boundaries of the old Roman Empire. These ten nations are of
Japhetic stock.

Japheth had a brother named Ham. Although they

were sons of Noah, Ham's descendants basically moved southward and spread over the continent of Africa. Japheth's offspring were in turn divided into fourteen nations, while Ham's descendants were divided into twice that number, thirty nations.

Shem, the remaining son of Noah, sired twenty-six nations who moved from their base at the foot of Mount Ararat eastward to become the vast continent of Asia. So we see three distinctive streams that sprang from the loins of father Noah, peopling the whole planet. On the fringe there were nations that can, for all intents and purposes, be regarded as mixed or hybrid nations. Examples of these mixed nations are found in Central and South America. Modern ethnologists classify the 192 national flags registered in the *1996 World Almanac* as having a basic association with one or more of these three principal races. Scientists classify them today as *Caucasoid,* or "European," *Negroid* or in the "African" category, and the *Mongoloid* or "Asian" group. A July 1997 U.N. membership report indicated membership at 185, meaning that some nations have not joined the world organization for one reason or the other.

Israel, The Hub

In considering the "end-time" scenario of nations as we know them today, we must focus in the center of the picture, the nation of Israel. Israel dominated the pages of both the Old and New Testaments. Israel is a part of the continent of Asia, although it bridges the three continents of Europe, Africa, and Asia. Americans need to be reminded that the nation of Israel belongs to the Shemitic rather than the Japhetic category. When we suddenly realize that 6 million Jews live as American citizens in the United States, we are prone to think of them as European or Japhetic. Though many Jews settled in Europe after the dispersion following A.D. 70, they are ethnically Asian, and therefore Shemitic. Jesus was a Jew, and an Asian, born in Bethlehem, Judah, Asia!

In these end-times it is fairly easy to recognize these three basic sets of Noah's descendants by tracing them to their roots as enunciated in our "Table of Nations and Languages" chart.

Let us take Israel, at the hub of the three divisions of nations, first. From the biblical point of view Israel is not only geographically at the center of the earth, but it is the one nation that God elected to become not His pet, but rather a pattern to the rest of the nations. The physical descendants of Abraham, Isaac, and Jacob, were "scattered . . . among the heathen . . . dispersed through the countries" (Ezekiel 36:19). This took place shortly after A.D. 70 when Titus sacked Jerusalem and destroyed the Temple. Now the dramatically significant thing is that this nation, at the core of the nations, was driven to the four corners of the globe nearly two thousand years ago. Suddenly in these end-times God has changed the picture. He promised these scattered people:

> I will take you from among the heathen, and gather you out of all countries, and will bring you into your own land.
>
> —Ezekiel 36:24

The nation, Israel, was gathered from 135 lands speaking 105 different languages, and now, since 1948, the Israelites are back in their Asian homeland, speaking their almost forgotten language of Hebrew!

Language Communication

In these end-times the seventy nations scattered at the

Tower of Babel are also being prodded into a single means of understanding and communication by language. One example of this reduction to one language is the sophisticated technology that has thrust the 192 national flags to a language they can understand by simultaneous translation. We read in Genesis 11:1 that "the whole earth was of one language, and of one speech." God changed that picture in Genesis 11:7–8:

> Go to, let us go down, and there confound their language, that they may not understand one another's speech. So the LORD scattered them abroad from thence upon the face of all the earth: and they left off to build the city [the Tower of Babel].

Now it has come full circle. By computerized electronic technology the nations of the earth can have the speeches at the United Nations building in Manhattan rendered simultaneously into a language they can understand. This is because the nations of the end-time are being gathered into alliances and confederacies. Take, for instance, the European Community of fifteen nations:

> "Eurotra"—an advanced language translating system—is being planned by the Community. In early June the Commission passed on the Council of Ministers a proposal for a research and development program for such a machine translating system. The communication also outlined a second action plan for improving information transfer between European languages. The first action plan was launched at the end of 1976. One of the most promising possibilities of it seemed to lie in introducing computer technology into multilingual activities and automating the trans-

lation procedure as far as possible. The Commission now has a terminology bank, "Eurodicautom," for instance, and machine-readable dictionaries for computer-aided or human translations. . . . It was found that the intelligibility of the machine-translated texts was exactly the same—98 percent—as for the same texts translated by hand.

—*Europe*, December 1980

This means that languages of these nations are being reduced to a common denominator by advanced electronic technology.

Eurodicautom

What is Eurodicautom?

Eurodicautom, created in 1976 by the Translation Services of the European Commission, is the Official and Technical Dictionary of the European Union. It is mainly a terminological database, containing scientific and technical terms, acronyms and abbreviations with their meaning, and not a generic dictionary. There's a Portuguese interface made by Pedro Moutinho, from the original one in English. However, access to it is only possible through the older version of this service. You see, a new interface has recently been created, although it is still experimental and does not have all features yet, it is much faster than the old one.

Who can take advantage of the service?

Eurodicautom provides translators, writers and researchers with an enormous set of scientific and technical terms in the official languages of the Community.

Features

This useful tool contains approximately 500,000 multilingual entries, that is, more than 2.5 million terms, as well as about 150,000 abbreviations and acronyms. It is updated every month, and 20,000 to 30,000 entries are added per year.

Sources

Eurodicautom was created with the available data of the Terminology Services of the European Commission and other European Union Institutions. Other sources were international organizations, national terminology centres, ministries, and professional organizations in the various Member States, and a range of specialist publications.

Languages

This service translates terms in 8 languages: Danish, Dutch, English, French, German, Italian, Portuguese, Spanish and in the near future, Greek.

Areas covered

Eurodicautom covers several areas related with the activities of the European Commission, such as European Union, administration, insurance, trade, economics, finance, law, atomic energy, environment, sciences, industry, building construction and civil engineering, mechanical engineering, transport, information technology, telecommunications, new technologies, agriculture, steel, mining, health and safety, etc.

How does it work?

In order to translate the word you are interested in, write it on the space provided bearing in mind umlauts and other special characters as indicated in the Special Char Translation Table. Then select from the 8 available languages the ones you wish as source and target languages. Click in "Start Query" and wait. Sometimes the service will not be available, as it may be being updated. . . .

Query results
The term, phrase or abbreviation sought is not simply translated. Besides the original term and its translation, you're given other data. Each record contains information on the date of record and reliability code from 0 to 5, where 5 represents standardized terminology. An extended research of all expressions in which the term occurs is automatically done. The available data is divided into items, both in the source and target languages, though not all of them appear for the term sought: key word, definition, reference, contextual sentence or phrase and explanatory notes (linguistic or technical).

How to access Eurodicautom
Access to Eurodicautom is free of charge, through Yahoo on the Internet if you enter the word *Echo*. As you do that, several entries will appear and all you have to do is click in Regional: Region: Europe: European Union: European Commission Host Organization—ECHO.

Direct access to Eurodicautom
If you want to find out more generic information, with links to other sites of interest, try: http://www.echo.lu/echo/databases/eurodicautom/en/eu92home.html

Your comments and suggestions are welcomed through Eurodicautom's E-mail.
—Internet, *www.letras.up.pt/transat/i_eurd.html*

The Western Confederacy

We have noted that with Israel's restoration in 1948 to nationhood and statehood, the characteristic of these end-times is an attempt to bring back into a single fold the nations that were scattered by God at the Tower of Babel. The United Nations, founded in 1945, now has 185 member nations on its roster. As the organization's name indicates, they are determined to unite under one ruler. They will not have long to wait. The Antichrist, to arise out of the revived Roman Empire, is being groomed to rule the world. Aligning the nations of the European Union is the first step to world hegemony. This is the end-time ten-nation western alliance described by Daniel as having "his feet part of iron and part of clay . . . and [ten] toes" (Dan. 2:33, 41–42; Rev. 13:1). This western confederacy is a Japhetic or European alliance. European Union members have a single passport, and all EU countries will have a single monetary unit, the Euro, by January 1, 1999.

The Northern Confederacy

Besides this "king of the west," there is also a "king of the north" (Dan. 11:40). The time factor is also indicated in Daniel 11:35: "the time of the end: because it is yet for a time appointed." The northern confederacy is also an attempt to align nations under a single world ruler in the end-times. However, this will never be achieved. This northern confederacy of nations is described in Ezekiel 38–39. The dominant member nation is, of course, Russia, called here, "Gog, the land of Magog" (Ezek. 38:2).

In our "Table of Nations and Languages" we have Magog described in Genesis 10:2 as being one of the "sons of Japheth." The Russian, or northern confederacy, is led by Japhetic hordes who are named as "Persia [modern Iran], . . . Gomer, [Germany], . . . Togarmah [Turkey]" (Ezek. 38:5–6). These are Japhetic nations, although Iran and Turkey are actually in Asia. Togarmah is listed in Genesis 10:3 as a "son of Gomer," as Gomer is listed in Genesis 10:2 as the eldest son "of Japheth." Persia is also linked with the Japhetic group, since Genesis 10:2 refers to Madai, the third son "of Japheth," who is the father of the Medes. His descendants settled as Iranic peoples south of the Caspian Sea. Of the six nations that comprise the specifically named northern confederacy, the aforementioned four—Russia, Germany, Turkey, and Iran—are ethnically Japhetic. However, in this named alliance two Hamitic nations are included: Ethiopia and Libya (Ezek. 38:5). The "Table of Nations and Languages" chart correctly lists the Ethiopians as being descendants of Cush, the first of Ham's sons (Gen. 10:6). The Libyans (Ezek. 38:5), however, are descended not from Cush, Ham's first son, but from Mizraim and from Phut (Put), the second and third sons of Ham (Gen. 10:6). Mizraim had seven sons according to Genesis 10:13–14, and the Libyans of North Africa, presently ruled by dictator Col. Muammar el-Qadhafi, spring from Lehabim. They are also descended from Phut whose offspring settled in Libya and Cyrenaica, North Africa.

So the northern confederacy is really a dominating alliance of Japhetic peoples who are the driving force behind the alliance and the secondary role of two Hamitic nations who cooperate with the Russian dominated alliance. Already Ethiopia and Libya have become the most pro-Russian nations in Africa. The monarchy under Emperor Haile Selassie I was overthrown in 1974, and the most powerful military African nation under Russian tutelage is today Ethiopia, occupying the vital and strategic Gulf of Aden through which all shipping must pass from the Orient to Europe via the Suez Canal. In 1969 Libya adopted a communist policy when Qadhafi seized power.

This ethnic distinction between the descendants of Noah's three sons can be seen. Iraq is listed in our chart as being a Semitic nation, while Iran is registered as a Japhetic nation. The Iraqis claim Iranians are not Arab, and Iran belongs to what is called today the Indo-Aryan, Indo-European, or Japhetic branch of nations.

We have already discussed Israel as the pivotal Shemitic hub of the nations, and we have examined the western confederacy today known as the European Union, all Japhetic nations. We have also analyzed the background of the northern confederacy with four Japhetic partners dominating the scene and two subordinate Hamitic partners. Now we turn to the eastern confederacy headed up by China, and "the kings of the east" (Rev. 16:12).

The Eastern Confederacy

The northern confederacy, headed by Russia, traced on a world map shows Russia as having the largest territory, 8.5 million square miles. When we come to the eastern confederacy, China has the largest population of any nation, 1.3 billion souls. According to Bible chronology, the Asiatic federation led by China will march into Mesopotamia in the latter half of the Tribulation. After crossing the Euphrates they will march against Israel. The Bible describes this vividly as follows:

> And the sixth angel poured out his vial upon the great river Euphrates; and the water thereof was dried up, that the way of the kings of the east might be prepared.
>
> —Revelation 16:12

The Bible describes "kings" rather than "a king." This means that there will be other Shemitic nations allied with China in this march westward toward Israel. Since China has the largest population of any nation on the earth, it is perfectly reasonable to concur with the numerical designation given us in Revelation 9:14, 16. After the sixth angel announces with his trumpet to "loose the four angels which are bound in the great river Euphrates" the "number of the army [is announced as] . . . two hundred thousand thousand." That would be 200 million. This would be one-sixth of the present population of China, registered as 1.3 billion.

This reminds us of the historic march of Genghis-Khan to the Middle East. His son Chagatai built the road through a ravine to the west. He had to break down the rocks of the slopes and build over forty-eight bridges. The Karakoram Highway from western China through to the Arabian Sea was completed as recently as June 1978. It writhes its way from the province of Sinkiang across the Himalayas to Pakistan, following Marco Polo's old silk route. Ten thousand Chinese coolies took eight years to hack their way over mountains eighteen thousand feet high. Twenty-seven hundred lives were lost in building it. It is known as "the new wonder of Asia" and has more appeal than the Great Wall of China. Moreover, in addition to this Karakoram Highway, the two Russian-built dams on the Euphrates River can now control the waters of that mighty river which is eigh-

teen hundred miles long. In 1974 the Keban Dam in Turkey was built by Russian engineers, followed by a larger
one in Tabqa, Syria, in 1975.

The *Sunday Times*, August 26, 1979, supported the
numerical prediction in Revelation by stating that China
can now mobilize 300 million guerilla fighters to counter
an enemy attack. The "kings of the east" not only include the Far Eastern and Southeast Asian nations, but
also the Middle East countries east of Israel. When you
add India, the second most populous country in the
world to the "kings of the east" you have another 800
million. These oriental countries spring from Shem.

The Southern Confederacy

Finally there is "the king of the south" (Dan. 11:5–20),
identified as Egypt, or as an Arab-African confederacy
dominated by Egypt. We are also instructed that "at the
time of the end shall the king of the south push" (Dan.
11:40). This confederacy is a Hamitic confederacy. The
Bible predicts that "Egypt shall not escape" (Dan. 11:42).
It further forecasts that "the land of Egypt shall be deso-
late and waste ... neither shall it be inhabited forty years"
(Ezek. 29:9,11). This Hamitic nation will evidently expe-
rience an atomic nuclear holocaust in the end-time.

Thus, we see all four confederacies—from the west,
north, east, south—converging toward the "hub," Israel.
Moreover in the upcoming battle of Armageddon, all
these nations arising from the original seventy nations
of Genesis 10, will become involved—the Japhetic, the
Semitic, and the Hamitic nations. We read in Zechariah:

> For I will gather all nations against Jerusalem to battle;
> and the city shall be taken, and the houses rifled, and
> the women ravished. ... Then shall the LORD go forth,

and fight against those nations, as when he fought in the day of battle. And his feet shall stand in that day upon the mount of Olives, which is before Jerusalem on the east, and the mount of Olives shall cleave in the midst thereof . . . and the LORD my God shall come, and all the saints with thee. . . . And the LORD shall be king over all the earth. . . .

—Zechariah 14:2–5, 9

Chapter 8

The Parade of Empires

The natural seeds of Abraham were in Egypt for four hundred years; in Israel under the judges for four hundred years; under the kings for four hundred years. Of course, the nation of Israel composed of ten tribes did not endure the full span of the last four hundred-year-segment, having been overrun by Assyria.

In approximately 600 B.C. the southern kingdom of Judah, composed mainly of the tribes of Judah and Benjamin (although some of all the tribes resided in Judah), was captured and plundered by Babylon, which had extended its empire from India to Egypt.

As prophesied by Isaiah, some of the young princes of the royal line of David had been taken to Babylon to serve in the court of the king, who was at that time Nebuchadnezzar. According to the account in the second chapter of Daniel, Nebuchadnezzar had dreamed what he thought must have been most important, but he had forgotten it. So he demanded of his wise men that they first tell him what he had dreamed, and then interpret it. The wise men failed, but God revealed to Daniel, a Jewish captive serving in the court, both the dream and the interpretation.

The king in a dream saw a huge idol, probably the

same size as that Nebuchadnezzar built in chapter three—six cubits wide and sixty cubits high. The head on the image was gold and doubtless looked like the king. The arms and breast were silver, the belly and thighs were brass, the legs were iron, with the feet partly of clay and partly of iron.

Daniel announced to Nebuchadnezzar: "Thou art this head of gold. And after thee shall arise another kingdom inferior to thee . . ." (Dan. 2:38–39).

Although the king built a replica of the image in pure gold from the head to the feet, his empire fell to the Medes and the Persians in 538 B.C. Babylon had invested too much of its wealth and manpower in military forces to keep the empire together. The Medo-Persian Empire controlled and dominated the nations between India and Egypt until in 333 B.C. Alexander annihilated the million-man army of Artaxerxes in western Turkey.

Although Alexander conquered all the nations within the Medo-Persian Empire, the monsoons, snakes, and malaria of the Indus River Valley were his greatest enemies. Finally, with a tattered remnant of his army, he made it back to Babylon in 320 B.C. and died a few weeks later. His empire was divided among his four generals. The gold empire fell; the silver empire fell; the brass empire fell; the last empire on Nebuchadnezzar's image was the iron empire.

This fourth world empire is described in Daniel 2:40–42, 44:

> And the fourth kingdom shall be strong as iron: forasmuch as iron breaketh in pieces and subdueth all things: and as iron that breaketh all these, shall it break in pieces and bruise. And whereas thou sawest the feet and toes, part of potters' clay, and part of

iron, the kingdom shall be divided; but there shall be in it of the strength of the iron, forasmuch as thou sawest the iron mixed with miry clay. And as the toes of the feet were part of iron, and part of clay, so the kingdom shall be partly strong, and partly broken. . . . And in the days of these kings shall the God of heaven set up a kingdom, which shall never be destroyed: and the kingdom shall not be left to other people, but it shall break in pieces and consume all these kingdoms, and it shall stand for ever.

The Word of God concerning the future of nations reveals that the Roman Empire would be broken into pieces, but when ten of the pieces formed an alliance at the end of the age, then the world would know that the coming of the Messiah to establish His own kingdom over the earth would be near.

Rome appeared as a world power in 242 B.C. with the conquest of Sicily. Gradually, the iron law of Rome was extended westward to Spain, northward to Germany and England, and eastward to Egypt and Syria. The Roman army under General Pompeius took protective custody of Jerusalem in 63 B.C., completing the replacement of Greece as the dominant world empire. The dominion of Rome over its conquered territories was as brittle and unyielding as iron in every respect. Taxes, goods, slaves, and produce flooded the markets of Rome from all over the known world. The citizens of Rome lived like kings, while the rest of the world lived like paupers.

Daniel, by inspiration of God, said:

And the fourth kingdom shall be strong as iron: forasmuch as iron breaketh in pieces and subdueth all

things: and as iron that breaketh all these, shall it
break in pieces and bruise.

—Daniel 2:40

In the chronological order of world empires, Rome, "the
iron kingdom," broke into pieces, with each piece becoming a nation. Rome has never ceased to exist; it simply broke up into independent nations. As the two legs
of iron represented Rome, the empire was divided into
two parts—the western division with Rome as its capital, and the eastern division with Constantinople as the
capital. The two legs stood side by side as one empire
until the iron empire began to break up in the year A.D.
476. The break occurred first in the right leg. The position of nations according to the Bible is as they face
Jerusalem. In A.D. 800, Charlemagne became emperor
of the Holy Roman Empire, and though he tried to heal
the split, he never quite succeeded. In the year A.D. 963
Italy was overrun by Germany, a province that Rome
had difficulty keeping under subjection. The Germans
then claimed the throne of the Roman Empire, and they
named their king "kaiser," which is German for "caesar."

The eastern division of Rome, and especially the
southern part, gradually succumbed to rising Arab nationalism as promoted by Mohammed from A.D. 570 to
A.D. 632. On his first military campaign into Asia Minor,
Mohammed brought back three thousand Christian
idols to Mecca. The churches of Asia did not heed God's
warning issued in the second and third chapters of Revelation, and their candlesticks were removed. However,
the capital of the eastern division of Rome was not conquered until A.D. 1453 by Mohammed II.

The Russians conquered and annexed much of the
northern half of the eastern division of Rome, includ-

ing Armenia. One historical source notes that Russians even occupied Constantinople for a time, and established St. Petersburg as the capital of eastern Rome. Eventually the capital was transferred to Moscow where it remains today. The Russians named their ruler "czar," which is Russian for "caesar." The Bolshevik Revolution, which was taken over by the communists, replaced the government of the Russian caesars by a system of commissars, or communist caesars. The board of communist caesars in Russia was presided over by a high caesar.

The relationship of the so-called "free world" with communism has gone through a series of changes—from allies, to direct confrontation, to peaceful coexistence, to detente, to *glasnost*, to the break up of the Soviet Union. The liberal propaganda has been that communism would mellow and change to a more yielding socialistic form of political ideology. However, Russia is one of the iron pieces in the leg of the Gentile image, and iron cannot change its shape except it be melted down and recast. The very symbols of communism are iron: the iron hammer, the iron sickle, and the iron fist.

Although the Soviet Union has been broken up into many republics along racial lines and traditional boundaries, there are still 20 million communists in Russia. Whether Russia will become a free market or semi-capitalistic country remains to be seen. Many believe it will revert again to a type of socialistic dictatorship. Ezekiel 38 and 39, which foretells a Russian invasion of Israel, will be fulfilled.

Daniel prophesied almost twenty-five hundred years ago that the Roman Empire would break into pieces and bruise. There have indeed been many such attempts, and as prophesied in the Bible, constant wars and bloodshed have resulted. The two greatest wars the world has ever known, World Wars I and II, began between nations of the old Roman Empire trying to put the image back together. However, before World War I, numerous attempts were made, and one of the most notable of these was made by Napoleon. Napoleon conquered all the western leg of Rome with the exception of England, and the emperor overran all the eastern leg of Rome with the exception of Moscow. He did occupy Moscow for a time, but he was not able to hold it. It was in Russia that he suffered a humiliating defeat from which his dreams for reuniting Rome never recovered. His vision was ultimately shattered at the battle of Waterloo in 1815, and history records that Napoleon's final defeat was due to an act of God. It simply was not time on God's prophetic calendar for Rome to be revived as the kingdom of the Antichrist.

After Napoleon, the next most serious attempt to weld together the pieces of iron was made by the kaiser, or caesar of Germany in World War I. Then came World War II when Adolf Hitler of Germany and Benito Mussolini of Italy formed the Axis alliance. Adolf Hitler made the same mistake that Napoleon made. He struck east at the old eastern leg of Rome, while leaving England, an unconquered portion of the western leg, and the United States, at his rear.

After World War II, Russia, which still possessed the relocated capital of eastern Rome, was presented with a golden opportunity also to capture the relocated capital of western Rome, Berlin. However, Berlin stood as the sole example of where the United States resisted communist pressure. It is reported that after World War II, Eisenhower had to threaten to use the atomic bomb against Russia in order to obtain the partitioning of Berlin. In this dividing of the city, the old capital buildings and sites remained in possession of the Allies instead of Russia. In spite of constant communist pressure, including the Berlin blockade, the United States stood firm. In May of 1975, Henry Kissinger, then secretary of state, went to Berlin to make a speech affirming the resolve of the United States to hold the German capital, even in the face of war.

Finally, the Soviet Empire crumbled from within and the satellite nations struggled to freedom. The Iron Curtain fell, East Germany was reunited with West Germany, and Berlin once more stood as the capital of what was once known as Germanic Rome. Perhaps few people on earth watching on television the tearing down of the Berlin Wall realized the prophetic importance of this dramatic event.

In returning to the dream of Nebuchadnezzar in Daniel 2, it is to be noted that the Iron Empire, or Rome, is the final Gentile empire. First, it was to be broken up in chunks, but even these chunks were to control the known world. The colonial system of world control grew up out of the break-up of the Roman Empire: the Dutch Empire, the Spanish Empire, the German Empire, the French Empire, the Belgium Empire, the British Empire, the Italian Empire, etc. India, Angola, Congo, South Africa, Australia, Canada, Singapore, Brazil, Ethiopia, Syria, Lebanon, Morocco, and dozens of other colonies around the globe were incorporated into the Roman colonial system. Indeed, Rome continued to control the world even in a fractured status.

Keep in mind that as the eyes of Nebuchadnezzar moved from the head of the image to the feet, he was also traveling in time from 600 B.C. to the time that the entire image would be destroyed. The iron part of the image began in about 200 B.C. It was still solid and unbroken at the time Jesus Christ was born, and it did not begin to break into chunks until approximately A.D. 500, a time span of one thousand years. The breaking of the iron legs began in about A.D. 500 and continued until A.D. 1945 through the Roman colonial system.

Now what change in the structure of the Gentile image occurred in 1945? The ebb and flow of changes in the boundaries of Europe changed, but not greatly, through the wars of the Hapsburgs, Napoleon, and the kaisers. However, in World War II a new idea came into the minds of world thinkers. There was going to be a revival of the League of Nations concept, a congress of all nations to meet and solve the problems and conflicts of mankind so there would be no more war. This common meeting place of the representatives of all nations was to be called the United Nations.

However, this plan for a world in which there would be freedom for all without fear of war called for the breaking up of the Roman colonial system. Joseph Stalin, Franklin Roosevelt, and Winston Churchill met at Yalta for a conference. Stalin and Roosevelt informed Churchill about their plan to break up the colonial system. Churchill protested that England had not fought, sacrificed, and suffered hundreds of thousands of casualties to the end that the British Empire be dissolved. Nevertheless, the prime minister of England could not prevent the prophecy of Daniel being fulfilled as prophesied in Daniel 2:41:

> And whereas thou sawest the feet and toes, part of potters' clay, and part of iron, the kingdom shall be divided; but there shall be in it of the strength of the iron, forasmuch as thou sawest the iron mixed with miry clay.

Nebuchadnezzar, as he moved in time down the Gentile image, saw the huge iron chunks becoming smaller and smaller until they were mixed with the clay of other nations. Indeed, the iron chunks of the Roman Empire did become smaller and smaller as colonies like Ethiopia, India, Egypt, Lebanon, Israel, Syria, Australia, Canada, Belgium Congo, etc., were broken off the European empires and became independent nations.

Jesus Christ prophesied of the refounding of Israel in the last days:

Now learn a parable of the fig tree; When his branch is yet tender, and putteth forth leaves, ye know that summer is nigh: So likewise ye, when ye shall see all these things, know that is in near, even at the doors.
—Matthew 24:32–33

However, Luke gave this prophecy of Jesus a more international interpretation:

. . . Behold the fig tree, and all the trees; When they now shoot forth, ye see and know of your own selves that summer is now nigh at hand. So likewise ye, when ye see these things come to pass, know ye that the kingdom of God is nigh as hand.
—Luke 21:29–31

After the refounding of Israel as a nation in 1948, all the trees began to bud. Nation after nation emerging from the colonial system gained independent status, but history of the past fifty years has proven that these are indeed clay nations, being pushed into various political shapes or social chaos by iron nations. It is an opinion held by many that the world would have been better off for most of these former colonies to have remained part of the European empires.

Daniel recalled to Nebuchadnezzar the conclusion of his dream in the toes of the image:

> And as the toes of the feet were part of iron, and part of clay, so the kingdom shall be partly strong, and partly broken.
>
> —Daniel 2:42

Which kingdom is still represented by the toes? The fourth kingdom, of course, because a fifth kingdom is not mentioned. Rome rose up out of western Europe, but it expanded to eastern Europe, the Middle East, Asia Minor, and North Africa. However, it is from its main source, western Europe, that the toes of the Gentile image are taking shape. On January 1, 1993, the EC became a single empire composed of twelve nations. Although these nations are still of the iron legs, they are mixed with a growing number of associate clay nations. The EC federation began in 1993 on a note of instability as two nations, England and Denmark, were still trying to keep the door open for a fast retreat in the event economic conditions dictated. The prophetic word of Daniel and Apostle John indicates there will be a solid union of ten nations when the leaders of these nations make up their mind to give all power to a single dictator (Rev. 17:13). England is of long-standing a democratic republic, and Denmark is reticent to lower its economic standards. The Danes are also fearful of the Roman Catholic Church. It is doubtful, from the date of this composition, that either nation is willing to surrender their government to a single authority. Only time will tell which ten European nations are willing to surrender all autonomy to a supreme monarch.

Also to be considered is the eastern leg of the Roman Empire (which became the Byzantine Empire), as well as Gomer's (Germany) involvement in the Russian invasion of Israel, as prophesied in Ezekiel 38 and 39. How can Germany be a part of the Common Market Empire and still join with Russia in a military venture into the Middle East?

It is evident from Daniel 2:42; 7:7; and Revelation 17:12, that when the Revived Roman Empire finally becomes solidified, it will be composed of ten nations. Luke quotes Jesus as saying that when the fig tree, or Israel, buds, and then all the trees bud, the "kingdom of god is nigh at hand." What kind of a kingdom was Jesus talking about? The same kingdom that Daniel saw that would end all Gentile rule and authority over Israel. "In the days of these kings shall the God of heaven set up a kingdom, which shall never be destroyed" (Dan. 2:44). Daniel recalled to Nebuchadnezzar's mind that in his dream he saw a huge rock strike the image on its feet and the entire colossus disintegrated into dust. Then, the Lord came and set up His own kingdom here on earth. The time frame for the end of the Gentile age is when Rome becomes one nation again. We are near that day, and most American Christians are still sleeping, although the prophetic alarm is screaming for them to wake up.

It is interesting that *Intelligence Digest*, the independent political and economic observer, calls the European Community a monster, or beast. Of the Revived Roman Empire, Daniel said:

. . . I saw in the night visions, and behold a fourth

beast, dreadful and terrible, and strong exceedingly;
and it had great iron teeth. . . .

—Daniel 7:7

There are many warnings about this growing monster
that is rising up out of the sea of humanity. From the
prophetic viewpoint, it will be interesting to see how it
grows and consumes all nations, races, and languages
(Rev. 13:7).

Chapter 9

The Parade of Four Beasts

To summarize the pre-written history of the Roman Empire in Daniel 2, Rome broke up into individual nations beginning with the sixth century A.D. In spite of numerous attempts at reunification from the time of Charlemagne to Adolf Hitler, the wars of Europe only resulted in massive bruising without accomplishing their intended purpose. However, with each attempt to reform the empire, a clearer picture of what will actually happen during the reign of Antichrist was presented. In the alliance of Hitler and Mussolini, a type of the union between the "political beast" and the "religious beast" of Revelation 13 appeared. Hitler became the greatest persecutor of the Jews ever to arise, and he even branded identification numbers on the forearms of the Jews. World War II lasted for six years (1939–1945), nearly the length of time given for the Tribulation period. Hitler sent his armies into North Africa to attempt the conquest of Jerusalem and the land of Palestine, and in this he almost succeeded. According to Bible prophecy, Hitler could have become the Antichrist, and those ministers during World War II who sounded the alarm that great signs concerning the soon return of Jesus Christ were in evidence, are to be commended rather than condemned.

However, we notice that the revival of Rome, as depicted in Daniel, is not to come about through war, but rather through a union of federated states. In the extremity of the toes on the Gentile image, the iron pieces are to remain separated and be mixed with clay when the Antichrist appears. As many Bible scholars have pointed out, in contrasting the clay with iron as relating to governments, the iron signifies military dictatorships and the clay represents democratic states, and even more likely, socialism, as we approach the end of the age.

It is important to our study to keep in mind that world power does not lie in Washington, D.C., Moscow, or Peking. World power is now centered in the Common Market of Europe, where it has been for the past two thousand years. Germany, fighting virtually alone, has almost conquered the world twice in one generation. Napoleon of France built the greatest army the world had ever seen to that time. If Europe had not been divided, Napoleon would have become a world ruler. The same is true of Kaiser Wilhelm and Adolf Hitler.

Nevertheless, the cohesive forces to hold the iron pieces of Rome together have been economics and religion. Marxism, which evolved into communism, came out of Germany through Karl Marx. Frederic Bastiat in 1848, in his book *The Law*, projected that communism and socialism from Europe would engulf the earth unless there was a return to the basic laws of God as set forth in the Ten Commandments.

From the most western nation of the old Roman Empire, England, socialism has spread as fast as Marxism did in Germany. The June 1975 edition of *Reader's Digest*, in an article entitled "The United States and the New World Society," made the following observation:

The notion of a world society is nothing new to America. . . . But there is something new in international pronouncements. . . . It is almost as if American opinion now acknowledged that there was no escaping involvement in the emergent world society. What happened in the early 1970s is that for the first time the world felt the impact of what I shall call the Bristish revolution which began in 1947 with the granting by socialist Britain of independence to socialist India. In slow, then rapid order, the great empires of the world—with the major exception of the former czarist empire—broke up into independent states; the original U.N. membership of 51 grew to 138. . . .

Socialist doctrine as it developed in Britain was that it was anti-American. More anti-American, surely, than it was ever anti-Soviet. . . . In the first half of the 20th century, British civil servants took the doctrine of British socialism to the colonies, a domain which covered one-quarter of the earth's surface. By 1950 not communists but Fabian socialists could claim that the largest portion of the world's population lived in regimes of their fashioning. . . .

The pieces which broke off the iron nation of Rome have indeed mixed with miry clay in the end of the age as prophesied. The United States finds itself in an emerging world society of socialism. As the author of the article in *Reader's Digest* suggests, our country is being carried along with the tide of our times to a new one-world order which has emerged through the economic and political policies which have risen in western Europe over the last century. One of the foremost organizations in our country which has directed this nation to that end is the Council on Foreign Relations.

The Common Market of Europe is not a new idea. It is simply an extension of the trade agreements which have kept the old Roman Empire together since the fifth century. A cookbook published by Doubleday on the history of food from ancient times to modern times had this to say about the Common Market of Europe:

> Fairs and markets were the light side of the Dark Ages and focal points of the burgeoning international economy. Caravans of merchants, minstrels, and peasants met seasonally to display and sell products ranging from songs and salted meats to rare spices and silks. Most famous were the fairs of Champagne near Paris held in the twelfth and thirteenth centuries. They lasted anywhere from sixteen to fifty days.

At the fairs and markets of Europe, princes and kings would meet to negotiate trade agreements. Naturally, political and religious matters entered into the deliberations. The revival of the Common Market of Europe today indicates the resumption of the old idea that if Rome is to be put back together again, it will be accomplished through peaceful economic cooperation rather than by military means. The sowing of the seeds of socialism and communism, both one-world political ideologies, has set the stage for the Revived Roman Empire to reap the harvest. The competition and controversy among the main four blocs of nations is only setting the stage for Rome again to rule the world.

In Daniel 7 we are given a description of four great world empires. These empires are called "beasts" because they devour much flesh.

> Daniel spake and said, I saw in my vision by night, and, behold, the four winds of the heaven strove upon the great sea. And four great beasts came up from the sea, diverse one from another.
>
> —Daniel 7:2–3

The Mediterranean Sea in the Scriptures is called the "great sea." As Daniel looked upon the sea, the four winds of heaven began to blow. The violent storm awakened four dormant monsters which came forth to prowl upon the earth, and all four beasts were predators— flesh-eating animals. Because the setting for this prophecy is in the night, it concerns the night of Great Tribulation. Winds are symbolic of spirit forces, and in the latter days it is predicted in the Bible that Satan would unleash devils and stir up the nations to war and rebellion against God (Rev. 16:12–14).

We read more about these four beast empires in Daniel 7:4–8:

> The first was like a lion, and had eagle's wings: I beheld till the wings thereof were plucked, and it was lifted up from the earth, and made stand upon the feet as a man, and a man's heart was given to it. And behold another beast, a second, like to a bear, and it raised up itself on one side, and it had three ribs in the mouth of it between the teeth of it: and they said thus unto it, Arise, devour much flesh. After this I beheld, and lo another, like a leopard, which had upon the back of it four wings of a fowl; the beast had also four heads; and dominion was given to it. After this I saw in the night visions, and behold a fourth beast, dreadful and terrible, and strong exceedingly; and it had great iron teeth: it devoured and

brake in pieces, and stamped the residue with the feet of it: and it was diverse from all the beasts that were before it; and it had ten horns. I considered the horns, and, behold, there came up among them another little horn, before whom there were three of the first horns plucked up by the roots: and, behold, in this horn were eyes like the eyes of man, and a mouth speaking great things.

The common interpretation of Daniel 7 is that the four beasts refer to the successive empires of Babylon, Medo-Persia, Greece, and Rome, as depicted in the Gentile world image of Daniel 2. However, we call your attention to Daniel 7:17: "These great beasts, which are four, are four kings, which shall arise out of the earth."

When Daniel interpreted the dream of Nebuchadnezzar concerning the image of Daniel 2, he pointed to the king of Babylon and said, "Thou art this head of gold." There was no question at all about Babylon's being the first empire represented in the image. However, in regard to the four beasts of Daniel 7 the prophet said that from his vantage point in history, these predatory animals representing four empires would arise in the future. Therfore, Babylon could not have been included as one of the beasts, because Babylon was a world empire at that time. It seems evident from the setting of the prophecy of the four beasts that it is in the latter years, the last generation of the age. It concerns four empires that will have vital interests in the Mediterranean area.

The first beast to appear is described as a lion with eagle's wings. The emblem of England is a lion, and the national emblem of the United States is an eagle. The Anglo-Saxon world of America and England ruled the

Mediterranean from 1918 to 1968. England ruled from 1918 to 1948, and the United States from 1948 to 1968, when Russia began to gain superiority over the Mediterranean Sea. The second beast is described as a bear, the well-known emblem of Russia, and, in accordance with the prophecy, Russia succeeded England and the United States as the predominant power in the Mediterranean Sea. The shift in the balance of power came in 1968 when the strength of the Soviet fleet began to exceed that of the U.S. 6th Fleet in the Great Sea.

The Soviet Union built the Aswan Dam in Egypt, and armed Egypt for both the 1967 and 1972 wars against Israel. The Soviets also armed Syria, intervened in Ethiopia, and most of the missiles and armor in Iraq's military machine were gifts from the Kremlin. Even though at the writing of this manuscript the "bear" may be hibernating, it is still keeping its paw in the Middle Eastern door.

The third beast is described as a leopard with four wings on its back, and it gains some measure of power over the Middle East through delegated authority. We read that dominion will be given unto it. According to Ezekiel 38 and 39, Russia will be defeated either just before, or immediately after, the Tribulation period begins. Thereafter, Russian influence in the Middle East is bound to decline or be eliminated altogether. The "leopard empire" is depicted as becoming dominant in the Mediterranean between the exit of the bear and the appearance of the fourth and dreadful beast. The leopard was adopted by the emerging African nations as their emblem for nationalism. We remember that the Mau Mau terrorists of Africa, who were in the forefront of the African nationalist movement, used leopard skins and claws in their attacks upon colonial rule and authority. The wings on the back of the leopard indicate delegated and protective authority from an outside source, possibly the United Nations. We quote from the article, "The United States and the New World Order," from the June 1975 edition of *Reader's Digest*:

> "We are now witnessing the emergence of a world order domination arithmetically by the countries of the Third World," said Daniel P. Moynihan, former U.S. ambassador to India. . . . Increasingly, the United States stands "accused and abased" before these nations. . . . While often hostile, these nations are not communist; generally, they are socialist. To date, their ideology has had limited force but, in the General Assembly of the United Nations and a dozen other such international forums, this new majority will set about to legislate "its presumed advantage in a world that has just come into its hands."

It may seem strange that world diplomats were talking about a "New World Order" in 1975. However, internationalists were preaching the New World Order after World War I, World War II, and through every United States presidential administration from Wilson to Clinton. President Bush simply made the nation more aware of the coming "New World Order" by popularizing the term through repetition. The New World Order won the war against Iraq; the New World Order is helping to restore order and resist anarchy in Somalia and Bosnia, etc. Such a United Nations force in the Middle East could be the leopard empire, or a Middle East alliance given backing by the United Nations. However, such a force or alliance is not to be confused with the world order that will be ushered in by the Antichrist.

The leopard is also a traditional symbol for Germany. East Germany and West Germany are again united as one nation. It has been commonly reported that an accord between Germany and Russia has been reached to further divide Czechoslovakia and Yugoslavia in the best interest of both countries. Germany is already in the process of absorbing divided Czechoslovakia, and Russia is profiting from the war in former Yugoslavia, plus increased loans from Germany. Germany (Gomer) and Russia (Gog) may certainly enter into a conspiracy as prophesied in Ezekiel 38 and 39.

We now come to the final Gentile authority in the Middle East and the Mediterranean area before Christ returns, the great and terrible beast with iron teeth and ten horns. The great majority of pre-Millennial Bible authorities identify this beast as the Roman Empire. The iron teeth identify the beast empire as an extension of Rome, and the ten horns stand for ten rulers who will be aligned with the Antichrist. It is the fourth empire that constitutes the kingdom of Antichrist. Out of the ten nations from the Roman Empire a president will arise to rule over the federation.

The following information is taken from the *European Economic Community* magazine, May 1979:

Right now, 410 carefully elected representatives from nine European countries are discussing the problems of the world. Their decisions could affect everyone on earth. Who is this select group? The new parliament of the European Common Market, jostling to become a world power. The Common Market is already the world's largest trading bloc, importing and exporting more than the United States and the Soviet Union combined. It has a population of 270 million, and a gross domestic product almost as large as the United States. January 1, the Common Market will add Greece as its tenth member. Already the accession agreement has been signed and the formal process of parliamentary ratification is taking place. As the Greek foreign minister put it, Greece will be an equal member of a huge democratic society of 270 million, with a political voice equal to that of the major European powers in the decision-making process.

As we consider the formation of a United Europe, it should be remembered that Daniel saw only four world empires rising up from humanity from the time of Nebuchadnezzar to the time of Antichrist. The fourth empire, Rome, while it did break up, continued to rule the world in its broken condition through the Roman colonial system. In the end of the age, represented by the foot of the image of Daniel 2, the large pieces were broken up into smaller pieces. These pieces of old Rome are still being broken up. We see this happening in Czechoslovakia and Yugoslavia. However, the fourth empire grows ten horns in the extremity of the age, and we read in Daniel 7:24:

> . . . the ten horns out of this kingdom [meaning the fourth kingdom] are ten kings that shall arise: and another [little horn—the Antichrist] shall rise after them; and he shall be diverse from the first, and he shall subdue three kings.

Although culturally, historically, and racially, the United States is tied to Europe, they are no friend, even though the United States has saved Europe twice in the twentieth century in World War I and World War II. Europe still remembers the Revolutionary War; the War of 1812; the Spanish American War; the Louisiana Purchase; Alaska; etc. To Europe the United States is still a barbaric nation and has despicable colonists.

Two professors at Cambridge in the 1880s completed revisionary work on the Textus Receptus which included the infusion of so-called older manuscripts which had previously been considered extra biblical and not divinely inspired. These professors were Westcott and Hort, and most of the newer versions (New King James Bible excepted) are based on the inclusions and revisions of these two men. While Westcott was more diplomatic than Hort when it came to overt editorializing, both basically agreed in both the political and ecclesiastical areas. One of the letters written by Professor John Anthony Hort to a constituent fairly well expresses the attitudes of Europe's majority regarding the United States, even today:

> I do not for a moment forget what slavery is, or the frightful effects which Olmstead has shown it to be producing on white society in the South; but I hate it much more for its influence on the whites than on the niggers themselves. . . . As yet everywhere (not in slavery only) they have surely shown themselves as an immeasurably inferior race, just human and no more, their religion forthy and sensuous, their highest virtues those of a good Newfoundland dog. . . . I care more for England and for Europe than for America, how much more than for all the niggers in the world! and I contend that the highest morality requires me to do so. Some thirty years ago Niebuhr wrote to this effect: Whatever people may say to the contrary, the American empire is a standing menace

to the whole civilization of Europe, and sooner or later one or the other must perish. Every year has, I think, brought fresh proof of the entire truth of these words. American doctrine destroys the root of everything vitally precious which man has by painful growth been learning from the earliest times till now, and tends only to reduce us to the gorilla state. The American empire seems to be mainly an embodiment of American doctrine, its leading principle being lawless force. Surely, if ever Babylon or Rome were rightly cursed, it cannot be wrong to desire and pray from the bottom of one's heart that the American Union may be shivered to pieces.

—Vol. 2, pg. 458—*Letters of Fenton*,
John Anthony Hort

At the writing of this book the European Union membership is fifteen nations. National boundaries are being erased and a common economic system based on the euro will be established by A.D. 2000.

The Maastricht Treaty projects that federated Europe will be in the final analysis a socialistic dictatorship. In fact, all the world will be forced into socialistic economics. Japan lost World War II, but it has won by winning the economic war with the United States through socialistic tactics—using trade to underwrite massive production, making it impossible for United States' business to compete in an open market. The same is true now in the European Union in countries like France subsidizing agriculture, and the Common Market acting together to underwrite forty percent of the Airbus' cost, throwing tens of thousands out of work in California and Washington. These socialistic practices in Japan and Europe are forcing new taxes in the United States to try to take care of the unemployed and stimulate business. However, each new tax increase brings our own nation nearer socialism, because that is what socialism is—taking money from the people to be spent by the central government. President Clinton is neither a Democrat or Republican—he is a socialist. The race toward socialism can be traced from Franklin Roosevelt to the present administration.

In looking toward a European socialist dictatorship of ten nations, we read in Revelation 17:12–13:

> And the ten horns which thou sawest are ten kings, which have received no kingdom as yet; but receive power as kings one hour with the beast. These have one mind, and shall give their power and strength unto the beast.

Eurocrats contend that this is the only way a Revived Roman Empire can come about—all nations belonging to the European Union must surrender all sovereignty to the central government. After this, the man who becomes dictator will take away three of the nations in the federation, or they will be absorbed by another nation or nations. Then, through economic power by all associate memberships, control the world and according to Revelation 13:16–17:

> And he causeth all, both small and great, rich and poor, free and bond, to receive a mark in their right hand, or in their foreheads: And that no man might buy or sell, save he that had the mark, or the name of the beast, or the number of his name.

Politically, economically, and ecclesiastically, the nations today are attempting to reverse what God did at Babel in dividing the nations. The United Nations, the New World Order, or the European Union are all manifestations of this vain imagination of men that will succeed for a little time.

Chapter 10

God's Controversy
with the Nations

God looked down through the ages and saw the time
when Satan would deceive the nations with another
Babylonish scheme: The dictator of a world government
would repeat the attempt made by Nebuchadnezzar to
command all nations and peoples to worship his image
as God or be killed.

Jeremiah 25:31–33 tells us:

> A noise shall come even to the ends of the earth; **for
> the LORD hath a controversy with the nations,** he will
> plead with all flesh; he will give them that are wicked
> to the sword, saith the LORD. . . . Evil shall go forth
> from nation to nation. . . . And the slain of the LORD
> shall be at that day from one end of the earth even
> unto the other end of the earth: they shall not be la-
> mented, neither gathered, nor buried; they shall be
> dung upon the ground.

Today Satan is stirring up the controversy between God
and the nations. We read in Isaiah 14:12:

> How art thou fallen from heaven, O Lucifer, son of

the morning! how art thou cut down to the ground, which didst weaken the nations!

Today Satan is weakening the nations through homosexuality, the sin that destroyed Sodom and Gomorrah. He is weakening the nations to prepare the way for the rise of a world government over which his own king, the Antichrist, will reign.

To illustrate again how near the world may be to this counterfeit kingdom, we refer you to the first fourteen verses of the twenty-first chapter of John. The scene described is by the Sea of Tiberias after the resurrection of our Lord. Eight of the apostles had been fishing all night with nets, but they had caught no fish. When Jesus appeared on the shore He instructed Peter to cast his net on the right side of the boat, and in verse 11 we read that they caught 153 fish.

There are no idle words in the Bible. All Scripture is given by inspiration and is profitable for doctrine, reproof, and correction, and the fact that John mentioned the exact number of fish must have an explanation. In the Bible, the gathering of the nations into the Kingdom, over which God's Son will reign from David's throne, is compared to the gathering of fish in a net. For example, we read in Ezekiel 32:2–4:

> . . . take up a lamentation for . . . Egypt . . . thou camest forth with thy rivers, and troubledst the waters with thy feet, and fouledst their rivers. Thus saith the Lord GOD; I will therefore spread out my net over thee with a company of many people; and they shall bring thee up in my net. Then will I leave thee upon the land . . . and will cause all the fowls of the heaven to remain upon thee. . . .

There are at least twelve scriptures relating to God's catching up the nations in His net; therefore, it is evident that the 153 fish the apostles caught in their net indicates the number of nations which will be on earth when the Lord returns. The entire mass of humanity is referred to as a "sea" in the Bible. We read in Daniel 7:2–3: ". . . the four winds of the heaven strove upon the great sea. And four great beasts came up from the sea."

Revelation 13:1: "And I stood upon the sand of the sea, and saw a beast rise up out of the sea, having seven heads and ten horns."

The beast referred to by John is the Antichrist and his empire that will rise up out of the sea. God will also cast His net into the sea and bring many fish (which represents the nations) to Armageddon. I believe that the 153 fish mentioned in John 21 represents the number of Gentile nations in the world when Christ returns, or at least the number of nations that will go into the Millennium.

At the close of World War II there were fewer than 100 nations, but with the breakup of the colonial empires the number began to rise. In 1966, when we first understood the meaning of the 153 fish caught by Peter and the apostles who were with him, we noted the count of nations had risen to 142.

Since 1942 nations have gained national status through the division of nations, or the emergence of new nations from the Roman colonial system, including the break-up of the Soviet Union. Also, some nations have lost their national status through the reunification of divided nations like East Germany and West Germany.

The apostles counted their fish and the total was 153. There was also a fish on the fire. The fish on the fire represented Israel during the last half of the Tribulation

(Zech. 13:8–9). Therefore, if our analogy is credible, then there will be 154 nations taken into the Kingdom Age.

In chapter 22 of 1 Kings we read that God had already determined how and where the wicked Ahab would be killed.

> And the LORD said, Who shall persuade Ahab, that he may go up and fall at Ramoth-gilead? . . . And there came forth a spirit, and stood before the LORD, and said, I will persuade him. And the LORD said unto him, Wherewith? And he said, I will go forth, and I will be a lying spirit in the mouth of all his prophets. . . .
>
> —1 Kings 22:20–22

Ahab's prophets gave him bad advice. He went up to the battle and was killed, and the dogs licked up his blood. Today the apostates, the ecumenists, the liberal educators, the humanists, and the one-worlders are giving the nations bad advice. Lying spirits are working overtime (Rev. 16:13–16).

What is happening in Israel and the Middle East today is the beginning of the final act in the drama of the ages. God is catching all nations into His net, and the times of the Gentiles will be brought to an end. The "goat" nations will be judged during the Kingdom Age and cast aside, and seventy nations will remain, in accordance with God's plan and purpose from the beginning.

The Parable of the Sheep and Goats

The eighth and final parable of the Olivet Discourse concerns the dividing of the goats from the sheep. Eight is the number of Jesus Christ, or the number of a new beginning. Therefore, we are given a hint that this parable looks beyond the Millennium to the new heaven and the new earth. We quote from Matthew 25:31–46:

> When the Son of man shall come in his glory, and all the holy angels with him, then shall he sit upon the throne of his glory: And before him shall be gathered all nations: and he shall separate them one from another, as a shepherd divideth his sheep from the goats: And he shall set the sheep on his right hand, but the goats on the left. Then shall the King say unto them on his right hand, Come, ye blessed of my Father, inherit the kingdom prepared for you from the foundation of the world: For I was an hungred, and ye gave me meat: I was thirsty, and ye gave me drink: I was a stranger, and ye took me in: Naked, and ye clothed me: I was sick, and ye visited me: I was in prison, and ye came unto me. Then shall the righteous answer him, saying, Lord, when saw we thee an hungred, and fed thee? or thirsty, and gave thee drink? When saw we thee a stranger, and took thee in? or naked, and clothed thee? Or when saw we thee sick, or in prison, and came unto thee? And the King shall answer and say unto them, Verily I say unto you, Inasmuch as ye have done it unto one of the least of these my brethren, ye have done it unto me. Then shall he say also unto them on the left hand, Depart from me, ye cursed, into everlasting fire, prepared for the devil and his angels: For I was an hungred, and ye gave me no meat: I was thirsty, and ye gave me no drink: I was a stranger, and ye took me not in: naked, and ye clothed me not: sick, and in prison, and ye visited me not. Then shall they also answer him, saying, Lord, when saw we thee an hungred, or

athirst, or a stranger, or naked, or sick, or in prison, and did not minister unto thee? Then shall he answer them, saying, Verily I say unto you, Inasmuch as ye did it not to one of the least of these, ye did it not to me. And these shall go away into everlasting punishment: but the righteous into life eternal.

This is another one of the parables of the Olivet Discourse that is greatly misunderstood and misapplied. The "social gospel" preachers of our day have taken it to promote so-called Christian socialism; that is, that the main responsibility of the Christian is to feed the poor and redistribute the wealth of the world. However, this is not what Jesus referred to in this teaching.

As in the other parables of the Olivet Discourse, Jesus gave a simple illustration using elements with which the apostles were familiar, and to which they could relate. They had witnessed the separation of the sheep and the goats many times. Goats and sheep were allowed to feed together during the day, but they were always separated at night. Sheep are placid animals, and at night they usually lie down and calmly rest until the morning. Goats are more aggressive and restless at night, so they had to be separated. Jesus took this simple illustration of separating the sheep and goats to teach the apostles what the Kingdom of Heaven would be like in respect to nations when He came again.

To find the meaning of this parable and its proper application, let us study it in its different divisions. We read first Matthew 25:31:

When the Son of man shall come in his glory, and all the holy angels with him, then shall he sit upon the throne of his glory.

Has Jesus come in His glory? Certainly not. During the Kingdom Age, all nations are to come up to Jerusalem to worship the King, and Israel is to be the head of the nations (Zech. 14:17–21; Isaiah 60:9–22).

During the course of the Kingdom Age, when nations are judged concerning their relationship to Israel, those that continue to rebel against the King's authority will be cut off, and those which follow Him and accept the leadership of Israel will be spared. We read in Matthew 25:40: "Inasmuch as ye have done it unto one of the least of these my brethren, ye have done it unto me."

I quote from *Dake's Reference Bible* concerning the explanation of this scripture:

> God will curse or bless according to how men have dealt with Israel. . . . This is the reason and basis for this judgment.

It seems apparent from Scripture that this judgment of the nations on the basis of their relationship to Israel, the Lord's brethren according to the flesh, will come at the end of the Kingdom Age, and not at the beginning. Those nations that are destroyed at the end of the Millennium will be those nations which have rejected Israel and Israel's King, the Lord Jesus Christ. We read in Revelation 20:9:

> And they went up on the breadth of the earth, and compassed the camp of the saints about, and the beloved city [Jerusalem]: and fire came down from God out of heaven, and devoured them.

We know from Revelation 20:1–7 that this will occur after the thousand-year reign of Jesus Christ as King of all nations. Those nations that are saved will inherit the new earth. We read of the New Jerusalem and the new earth in Revelation 21:24:

> And the nations of them which are saved shall walk in the light of it [New Jerusalem]: and the kings of the earth do bring their glory and honour into it.

There is a growing awareness in the world that the nations are headed toward a rendezvous with destiny, caught up in a whirlpool of situations that are irreversibly sweeping them into a single vortex. National problems become international problems, and then international problems become national problems. Many experts believe that the human race has passed the point of no return, and the only hope is to burn our bridges behind us and plunge on into the future because there is no other course open. An article by F. M. Esfandiary, who teaches long-range planning at the University of California at Los Angeles, advocated this point of view in the *Houston Chronicle:*

> In just the last 10 years, we have learned more about our genes and brains, about our planet and resources, and the solar system, than in all previous history. And we are only beginning. . . . Powerful forces are revolutionizing life on the planet. Decades from now, the 1980s will be remembered as a time when the world accelerated toward a new age. . . . The centralized, bureaucratized infrastructures and congested cities of the industrial age are becoming increasingly superfluous. They will give way to teleducation, telemedicine, electronic funds, teleshopping, teleconferencing. You connect from wherever you are. . . .

Parents no longer exercise unilateral influence over their children. . . . It matters less and less who is legislator or president. The driving forces of change are increasingly outside government. . . . We cannot switch to new technologies and new resources while holding on to traditional values, the nuclear family, puritan morality, the work ethic, patriotism. No Moral Majority or tradition-bound administration can now stop or even slow down the cumulative, interlocking impact of social and technological advances.

Professor Esfandiary contends that it makes no difference who we elect to the presidency or Congress; it makes no difference whether or not the churches object to the new morality; it makes no difference what the preachers preach; it makes no difference what the parents teach their children—forces already set in motion will determine the future. We now know how Noah must have felt when he preached to his generation without any visible results, and Jesus said that this would be the way it would be again in the last days.

We are witnessing this Antichrist system taking shape before our eyes, but Jesus is coming back to destroy it with the brightness of His coming. God, who divided the nations and set the bounds of their habitation will see His plan and purpose fulfilled.

Every person who has not already been born again by faith in Jesus Christ is faced with two choices. He may believe on Jesus Christ, who died for the sins of mankind, and be saved, or he may reject the message of Christ. To turn from Christ is to risk dying in sin and possibly living to face all the terrors of the Great Tribulation, with its wars, earthquakes, famine, political and economic upheaval, disease, and misery. To reject Christ is to face all eternity without God and without hope.

The study of prophecy has two major purposes: (1) to encourage those who have trusted Christ to be about the urgent business of bringing people to Christ, and (2) to encourage those who have never trusted Jesus to accept Him as Savior and Lord. Paul wrote:

> . . . If thou shalt confess with thy mouth the Lord Jesus, and shalt believe in thine heart that God hath raised him from the dead, thou shalt be saved. For with the heart man believeth unto righteousness; and with the mouth confession is made unto salvation.
>
> —Romans 10:9–10

We could be living in the last century. In fact, Jesus could call away the believers today. Are you ready?